A Combat Medic

Comes Home

John Kerner, M.D.

iBooks

Habent Sua Fata Libelli

iBooks
1230 Park Avenue
New York, New York 10128
Tel: 212-427-7139
bricktower@aol.com • www.BrickTowerPress.com

Library of Congress Cataloging-in-Publication Data

Kerner, John.
A Combat Medic Comes Home
p. cm.

1. Biography. 2. Medical—History. 3. Women's Health. 4. World War II
Nonfiction, I. Title.

ISBN-13: 978-1-59687-937-9, Trade Paper

September 2012

A Combat Medic

Comes Home

John Kerner, M.D.

DEDICATION
For my wonderful wife Gwen—my best friend.

Contents

Chapel for the 359th Division in Normandy

Foreword

My wife, Gwen, took a message from a man in South Carolina for me to please call him. His first words to me were, "You saved my life." After all these years since World War II, he had, at last, found me. He finally got a clue when he got hold of a book I had written, *Combat Medic, World War II*. In it he found that I had changed my name from Kapstein to Kerner after the war. Now he could locate me.

He told me that a land mine had blown off the lower portion of one of his legs. I had gone to his aid under difficult circumstances, stopped the hemorrhage and got him out.

Interestingly, I remembered it all. I had not thought of that time for over sixty years.

Shortly after my division, The 35th, landed on Omaha Beach in the invasion of Normandy, I was moved from a collecting company to take command of a battalion aid group, 2nd Battalion, 320th Infantry. The two doctors who had been in command were both casualties. Very shortly after I took command I was on the road through the hedgerows getting ready to set up an aid station. We saw a man lying in the middle of a small field. He was obviously in great distress. Someone had set up a crude sign: "BEWARE MINES." Up to that time, we had not come across mines, though we knew a bit about them. My aid men hesitated because they thought that this was a trap. I thought I should see what I could do. I crawled out with my aid sack toward the man in distress, looking carefully at the ground to see signs of a mine, though actually, at that point, I had never seen one. I marked part of my way with bits of white gauze.

When I got to the man, he was bleeding briskly from one of his legs and his foot and some of his lower leg were held on only by a small bit of skin. I cut the blown-off segment free and applied a pressure dressing using Ace bandages. (Such bandages were not G.I., but I had obtained a supply for my men. This was the first time I had used one in the field.) I gave the man a shot of morphine and dragged him out the way I came in, I hoped. By that time the aid men who were with me helped. We put the injured man behind a hedgerow, started some plasma I.V., and gave him a cigarette. We had a ambulance nearby to which we took him on my jeep on a litter held in place on the hood by clips my men had designed. That was the last I heard of that man until this phone call.

In retrospect, that was an important event in my life, because up until that time my aid men were uncertain of me. I had had no field experience and was in combat with minimal training. I began to get some respect from my men and for myself—which I think led to many of the events in this book.

Chapter 1

Return to Training, January 1946

Still on terminal leave, I was assigned to the San Francisco General Hospital as assistant resident in obstetrics and gynecology. The war had recently ended and I had hardly begun to feel like a civilian. I still had nightmares related to combat in Europe. While walking in Chinatown with my new girlfriend, Gwen, someone set off a string of firecrackers. The next thing I knew, I had ducked into a doorway, leaving Gwen walking down the street by herself. It would take a long time to forget the things I had done to stay alive during 222 days of combat.

The "General" is a huge city hospital and usually filled close to capacity. It boasts a superb emergency service. The University of California Medical School had a busy obstetrical and gynecologic department there. I had been in the Army for two years, most of that time as a combat medic, with a brief stint in plastic surgery just before I was discharged. I had served little more than an internship before I left on short notice for the Army. My professor, Herbert Traut, had promised me a position when I returned from the war. I do not think he considered that there was a good chance that I would not make it back.

The head resident at the General was Neal Elzey. He had been released from service recently, having served much longer than I did. He was desperately overworked. The obstetrical service was busy, the birth rate had gone up with the end of the war, and women with gynecologic problems filled a whole ward. A major problem was severe pelvic infections brought on by criminal abortions. Abortion was illegal at that time. We had a very small amount of antibiotic available, which made the care of these unfortunate women difficult.

After I had been at San Francisco General for about a week, Neal let me handle our emergency service while he took a much needed night off. My consultant was Daniel Morton, a doctor idolized by trainees in our department. During the early evening, I supervised two deliveries done by an intern. I was just getting ready to go to bed after checking the women's ward when I got a call from the emergency room.

There was a woman with a bullet hole in her lower abdomen. She was about eight months pregnant. The emergency room physicians thought they heard a fetal heartbeat, though it was not normal. I told them to crossmatch some blood and get her to surgery as quickly as possible. I called Doctor Morton. He said to go ahead and do a cesarean section and that he would be along soon to supervise. We wanted to control internal bleeding and to save the baby if possible.

I had never done a cesarean section and no abdominal surgery since just after I entered the service, and what I had done before that was minimal. I had seen cesarean sections during my internship, but that was over two years before. I asked one of the interns to give me a hand. By the time I got to the operating room an anesthesiologist was there, and the experienced nurses had set up for an emergency laparotomy. As the patient was being prepped, I noted a small hole in her abdominal wall below the umbilicus. There was no external bleeding. I used some local anesthetic to protect the baby, made an incision, exposed the uterus, and had the anesthesiologist give some Pentothal. That allowed a short time to deliver the baby. I made an incision in the uterus and delivered the baby with a good quantity of blood in the uterine cavity. The baby responded, though weakly. It was pale. A pediatrician who had arrived took over the baby. I found the hole in the uterus and noted that the lower portion of the placenta had been torn; that was the source of blood loss. The bullet was in the uterine cavity and had not gone out the posterior side. In a sweat, I delivered the placenta. I looked at the incisions I had made. Doctor Morton's quiet voice came from the observation gallery. He instructed me how I should close the uterus after being sure that it would drain. Closing the abdominal wall proved to be no problem. The baby, though small and weak, survived. All of this took a short time, but I was exhausted. A compliment I got from Doctor Morton was worth a military medal.

Now I was really ready for bed. But I was called by the intern on duty to supervise his delivery of a woman in labor whose baby was in breech position. Fortunately, it was her third child. By the time I got to the delivery room, the delivery had started and I instructed the intern. Now I was truly back from the war.

I was at rounds at eight o'clock the next morning. Doctor Morton came early and we were expected to be there with full knowledge of all the patients. Our cesarean section patient was doing well, but there were major problems on the wards. Fortunately, Neal was back and the work could be spread out a bit.

We had a little penicillin, but special permission was required to use it. Sulfa drugs were used, but they were not effective against the infections of complicated abortions. The result was that we had to operate on many of the young women and, unfortunately, they often ended up sterile. They spent long periods of time getting well enough for surgery and more time to recover.

Though the service was busy, most of the surgery was done by the senior resident. That left the assistant resident to supervise obstetrics, teach medical students and interns, assist in surgery, and do minor surgery. I wanted to do more surgery, so I prowled the hospital looking for cases. It was agreed that if I found a candidate, I would be given a chance to do the operation with supervision.

On a medical ward, I found a post-menopausal woman with a hugely distended abdomen. The diagnosis in her chart was ovarian cancer with metastasis to the lung. She had a difficult time breathing. Her chest contained a large amount of fluid. Her abdomen had a large tumor and it also was surrounded by fluid. She was on the medical ward to die. Doctor Morton said that I could do the operation if I would use only local anesthesia.

The tumor, which weighed nine pounds, was attached minimally, and I was able to remove it. It was benign, a fibroma. The fluid that had developed in the abdomen and chest cleared. The patient, who had been bedridden, was able to get up with help the next day and made a rapid recovery. The final diagnosis was Meigs syndrome with an ovarian fibroma. This woman's case taught me a vital lesson: we should never give up unless we are sure that there is nothing constructive that we can do beyond keeping the patient comfortable. For about twenty years after the surgery, I received a box of homemade cookies from the patient every Christmas.

I found it difficult to convert from the relative independence of my position in the military to the discipline of the hospital training program. I had had the responsibility for training aid men in the Army, but I had been away from a hospital training program for two years, living in an entirely different environment.

I had pictured my training in obstetrics and gynecology as it had been before the war, but there had been significant changes. Prior to the war there were few specialists with formal post-internship training. It was planned that the university-trained, post-internship residents would be consultants for general practitioners. The war changed that because the armed services gave special rewards to qualified specialists. Such qualification usually required at least three years of postgraduate training. Those rewards were reflected in higher rank, better positions, and a chance for doctors to perform their specialties. Returning veterans were eager to become specialists. Consequently the universities had to prepare to enlarge their teaching programs. Medicine in the United States changed; people began to demand qualified specialists even for normal births and other common problems.

At the University of California Medical School, Herbert Traut, the chairman of the Department of Obstetrics and Gynecology, enlarged his program by adding hospitals outside of the university hospital to the training program. This made space for returning veterans. The new hospitals, at first, included St. Mary's and St. Luke's. He gave selected members of those staffs clinical ranks in the Department of Obstetrics and Gynecology at UCSF. Residents were to be rotated between the various hospitals until they had three years of training and achieved the rank of senior resident.

When I was notified that after six months at San Francisco General I was to go to St. Mary's, I was upset and complained that I had expected a residency at the university hospital. Doctor Traut called a meeting of all trainees and said in no uncertain terms that he was in charge, and that he would decide how we would be trained. So much for what I had thought I had earned in many months of combat.

I was called up for active duty by the U.S. Army on December 24, 1943.

I had expected to be deferred until my training was complete. I was told to leave for basic training on December 26, before I had completed my internship in Obstetrics and Gynecology. It had been difficult for me to break the news to my family and a girlfriend, Chris. On the other hand, we all felt that because I was top student, I would probably be assigned to a hospital somewhere. Little did we know that I would be with combat troops in the invasion of Normandy and to the end of the war.

I had a wonderful family who were thrilled to have me home. They had a difficult time accepting the fact that for quite a while after my return I was depressed. The readjustment was not easy. My father was a self-made man who had gone to work at an early age for a Massachusetts company called E.P. Charlton. This company merged with Woolworth, which my father helped develop before going on to start his own variety stores. He worked hard and rarely questioned what his children were doing. As a result, we were quite strong as individuals. My mother was an attractive woman who, finding all of her children out of the house, decided that she should be in business. While I was away, she became a nationally known interior designer. My sister Dorothy, the brightest of three children, was four years older than I, and had four children—Julie; Renee and Jeanne, twins; and the youngest, Nick. As a student in medical school I often babysat for these kids. I was fond of them. My sister's husband Henry was from a French family. We all enjoyed his sophistication, which was matched by that of my sister. My brother Bob was a remarkably good student who entered college at an early age. He received a Naval commission as an ensign and was sent to Harvard Business School, and then to the Pacific island of Saipan to manage supplies for the Navy in that area. I had seen him briefly while we were both on leave.

I had set myself up at the General, which we usually called "the County." Since there were many births, I spent my nights in the obstetrics wing. That wing had just been completely rebuilt; however, a major error had been made. The doors of the rooms did not permit a gurney or a bed to fit through. This resulted in our not being able to use a whole new ward. Since it was empty, I took over two rooms for living quarters. There was no phone on this ward, so I rigged up a long cord going down to the nurses' station at labor and delivery. At my end of the cord I had a noisemaking device. If the nurse wanted me she pulled on the cord, and I would run down the stairs. Though this setup was in some ways primitive, I did have the luxury of two rooms, and it was possible for people to visit me. I had been depressed in part because of the abrupt change from combat to seeing life had gone on in San Francisco with little change. Chris was away at school in Oregon. I did go out and walk around a bit. In her practical way, my mother suggested that I get out and make some dates. I called the most attractive young women I had known before the war, and one or two suggested by my sister. I still had a great deal of money, and my father, as always, was generous in his offers to provide more if I needed it.

The dates, though lovely young women, were boring. These girls had not done much in relation to the war effort. They had been in college, but did not seem smart to me. We usually went dancing. Some danced better than others. There was one, Meta, whom I did like, but she seemed to be already taken. In general these young women were looking for husbands, not careers. They did not understand what war was about, and I was not about to tell them. A couple of days before I had to return for duty prior to discharge, I agreed to a blind date. A good friend of my parents "knew a girl who would be great for John to meet." My family knew her family, though not well. Her father was a busy lawyer. Her family lived in St. Francis Wood, a nice residential area across the city. I had resisted a number of blind dates, but for some reason I thought I would give this young woman a try. Gwen lived in a lovely Spanish-type home, which was approached through a nice patio with flowers growing all around. She met me at the door, and I was struck by her good looks. She was about five feet two, with long, brown hair and blue eyes set in a lovely face. We went dancing at The Mark Hopkins Hotel on Nob Hill. I got a table near the dance floor. I ordered a Scotch and water; she ordered a soft drink. I suggested that she try a bourbon and ginger ale. She did not usually drink except when her father made old fashions on special occasions, but she ordered a bourbon and soda, and seemed to like it. She was a bright woman, a Stanford Phi Beta Kappa. At that time there were not many women who made that society. She danced like a dream. That was a special pleasure. Though I was only a fair dancer, I loved dancing. It had been years since I had danced with anyone who was really good. Gwen worked for the state in a secretarial job. That, too, was unusual, since none of the girls I had known in San Francisco worked, except for those at the hospital. I felt at ease with her, and something told me that she could well be the girl for me. After all the women I had met at home and overseas and after all my experiences, this woman seemed to me to be the ideal companion—for life. She wrote regularly when I returned to duty briefly, awaiting discharge. Of course it was a pleasure to have her join me for dinner, even if it was in the cafeteria.

My parents had minimal room for me in their apartment, so I was inclined to spend a good deal of time at the hospital. This relative luxury was to be given up when I moved to St. Mary's, where I had a small room in the house staff quarters.

St. Mary's was a pleasant surprise. It was run with great efficiency by Catholic sisters. It had the most active obstetrical service in San Francisco, and there were a number of first-rate obstetricians, including Charlie Mohun and Gerry O'Hara. Those men and others let me do many of their deliveries, with them supervising. I got to do a large number or repairs of incisions and tears, and was also taught the use of forceps. I finished my training being outstanding in forceps use, which was to prove invaluable. Mohun and O'Hara were doing over eighty deliveries a month, and one of them slept in the hospital each night. They were wonderful role models. Phil Arnot, who was one of UCSF's first residents, also worked at St. Mary's. He had remarkable instincts and anticipated difficulties better than anyone I had ever worked with. He was supportive of residents and gave wonderful parties for members of the department in his lovely home in St. Francis Wood.

While I was still at the County, Gwen and I were secretly engaged, but it was not a secret for long. Sometime before I went into the service, my mother had the diamond from her engagement ring mounted in a black iron ring, which she gave me for my birthday. I wore that ring through the war, and by the time the war ended the inner side of the ring was worn almost through. The stone was perfect for a ring for Gwen. I went to Laykin's, a jewelry department in I. Magnin. They had done work for my family. Their designer produced some unusual designs and I chose one which was of gold with four posts, the diamond set between them. It was beautiful and quite unusual at the time, when most engagement rings were of the classic Tiffany style. The setting was a bit expensive for me, and I wondered if Gwen would be happy with a non-traditional ring. The jewelers kindly asked me what I had planned to spend, and they settled for that, knowing I would return as a customer.

Back in the United States, waiting to fly home

Woodcome, me, and Cook
Dressed for the bitter cold near Bastogne

V.E. Day

Aid Station Crew
Second Battalion, 320th Infantry

My truck outside of Bastogne

Chapter 2

Herbert Traut, January 1947

It was time to return to the University of California Hospital. My assignment as a second-year resident was primarily to be an assistant to the chairman, Herbert Traut. I was responsible for all the pathology reports and, if necessary, to have them corrected by Daniel Morton; all postmortem examinations for our department; slides of all tissues removed in surgery; assistance at every lecture Doctor Traut gave that included operating the projector. In addition, I took my turn on call at night and for emergency surgery. It was a great opportunity to expand my knowledge. The position required that I put in long hours of work and study, but my new bride Gwen understood. We had been married on June 16, 1946. We had a lovely wedding at the Mark Hopkins Hotel, with a reception there. We were permitted a brief honeymoon in Santa Barbara.

Herbert Traut was only the second chairman of a fully organized training department at UCSF. His predecessor, Frank Lynch, had been chairman for close to thirty years. Traut was a superb choice. He had been trained in gynecology and obstetrics at Johns Hopkins, and he also had a formal residency in general surgery at that institution. He had gone to Berlin to study with the world's foremost gynecologic pathologist, Robert Meyer.

Traut was a big man with thinning blond hair, and he wore glasses. He was a strict disciplinarian and a great teacher. From Hopkins he went to Cornell Medical School, where he was associate professor of obstetrics and gynecology, but his particular interest was gynecology and its pathology. It was from that post that he was chosen to chair the department at UCSF.

Not long before he came to San Francisco, Doctor Traut wrote a monograph with George Papanicolau, "The Diagnosis of Uterine

Cancer by Vaginal Smear." At that time, cancer of the uterus, particularly of the uterine cervix (the vaginal portion of the uterus), was a major cause of death in women the world over. Diagnosis had been made by biopsy, called for by changes in the cervix noted on speculum examination or by abnormal bleeding or discharge. Their concepts held some interest in professional circles, but they were hardly accepted. Traut's colleagues insisted that the only approach to diagnosis was with biopsy. But it was not always clear who to biopsy and from which areas to get specimens. This led to multiple biopsies, many of which were not necessary. Traut was convinced that the smears would make it possible to find the patients who needed biopsy, and further, he felt cancer could be found in its earliest forms, perhaps in its precursor form. He set out to educate the profession. It was not easy; he needed proof. He called me in and showed me smears with cells that he was convinced were cancer cells mixed with other cells. He assigned me the task of finding where the cells came from, which often required multiple biopsies and then looking at them through a microscope to find those cells that matched the abnormal ones on the smears. The unusual cells came from cancerous or precancerous areas. Having done that, I was then asked to make projector slides of smears that showed the abnormal cells, and then make slides of the area of the uterus from which the cells came. This was a major challenge. At that point no projection slides had been made of vaginal smears, and projection slides of other tissues were of low magnification. Vaginal smears needed high power to show the nature of the cells.

I found that there was one technician in hematology who had been working on making photographs of blood smears. Blood cells were about the same size as the vaginal smear cells. I sought out this technician, a pleasant woman working with Stacy Mettier. We would find a slide that I had collected from our clinic. I would select the cells that I wanted to use as an illustration. That cell or group of cells was put under the highest-power oil immersion lens of our microscope. We then took off the eyepiece of the microscope and fastened a camera in its place. First, we had to design a way for the camera to fit. Then we had to find a camera lens that could duplicate what the eyepiece did. We finally accomplished all of that and got suitable pictures. An equally difficult assignment was to make photographs of positive biopsies and the smears that showed cells similar to those that indicated the biopsies were abnormal. Finally, after months of work, I had a set of slides for the professor. He came through with one of his rare congratulations, and put the slides to work at local and national meetings. Interestingly, when I finished my training almost two years later, the technique was still not accepted by most pathologists, who continued to feel that uterine cancer could only be found by biopsy. One of my first jobs was to travel the state under the auspices of the American Cancer Society to promote the value of the vaginal smear. It gradually came to be accepted, and few discoveries of modern times have saved the lives of so many women. The smear had made it possible to find early cancer and even precancerous disease of the uterus. By early detection, it became possible to cure the disease in over 90 percent of patients with simple surgery or freezing, without having to subject those women to radical surgery, irradiation, or both.

During this phase of my education I worked a good deal with the chief of pathology at UCSF. He was much interested in the work I had done, and he began using photography through the microscope. He also was the first pathologist besides Traut and Papanicolau to foresee the value of the vaginal smear. He also began to make smears of the respiratory tract and the urinary tract, but they proved to be much less reliable than the vaginal smear. All our original work was in black and white. There was an interval before we could use color.

From all this work with vaginal smears and the associated biopsies, I developed a lifelong interest in cancer diagnosis and treatment. My interest was later stimulated by the fact that my sister, mother, and father all died from cancer.

While doing this work at UC, important personal events developed. Shortly after we were married, Gwen, my brother, and I decided to change our last name from Kapstein to Kerner. Gwen and I anticipated having children, and we felt that they would have fewer problems in life with a name that did not carry with it indication of religious background. I had found that in our Army there were widespread prejudices. African-American soldiers were not treated as equals. In almost all cases they were in separate units commanded by white officers. Yet they did exemplary service. The Red Ball Express was an excellent example. That was a unit of black truckers who brought supplies to us as we advanced from the beach in Normandy. We worked with an excellent tank outfit in which the highest-ranking black man was a noncommissioned officer. Jews fared a little better, but there was widespread anti-Semitism. I noted that Jewish officers rated as "superior" often were passed over when advancement in command was available. In most cases, the Army could not avoid promoting combat officers who put in their time; however, the best positions rarely went to Jews. That experience led me to change my name. I did not want my children to face that sort of prejudice. My first child, John, was born in 1947, and his name was John Alan Kerner Jr. It was fortunate that John's birth came at a time in my training when there was less structure. That gave me more time to be a support for Gwen. When we were first married, the only suitable apartment we could find was one just being completed not far from the County and U.C. Hospital. When Gwen became pregnant, we knew we would need more space. We joined a group of our friends and bought an apartment building with six units for $60,000. It was in a nice area and was relatively spacious. We only had to put $500 down because we all got G.I. loans.

* * *

As part of our therapy for most cases of cervical cancer, we placed radium in various containers around the diseased areas. The time it was left in was carefully calculated, and that often meant that it had to be removed at odd hours in the night by tired interns or residents. Certain of the radium containers were held in place by gauze packs. Others were in rubber tubing into which small containers of radium were placed, and these were inserted into the cervical canal (the canal into the uterus through the cervix). When not in use, the radium was placed in a safe, since it was extremely valuable. One day, when the head resident went to check the radium for the following day, he found some of it missing. These missing sticks had been in a rubber tube. The alarm went out. We scoured the treatment room where the radium had been removed. There was none to be found, and the packing had been taken away. We got Geiger counters, which click in the presence of radiation, and searched everywhere on the ward and the treatment room. Not one click. We then went to the waste collection area of the hospital. No clicking there either. We then thought that if the radium had mixed in the packing, it would go to the incinerator, so we went to it. This was Sunday. Debris from Saturday had been incinerated. The ashes had been carted away. We found out the ashes were dumped in a city landfill. We equipped the house staff with all the Geiger counters available. We calculated where it was most likely that the debris from UC would have been dumped and spread out to search. Skip was the first to pick up a click. We rushed over to the area and to our joy found all three of the missing capsules of radium. In our anxiety to get them back, I am sure we all got too much exposure to irradiation. All the radium was returned to the safe where it belonged. No one reprimanded the house staff member who had made the mistake. We never told the senior staff of the event. Radium was never lost again.

Alice Maxwell, who was a full professor, left the faculty. She had felt that the position of chair should have been hers. She was an outstanding physician, a fine teacher, a great surgeon, and highly respected by all who knew her. She was beautiful and had great presence. When she came in to give lectures, the students would all stand. They gave that honor to no other professor, She had worked with Doctor Lynch and was one of his first faculty appointments. At department meetings after Doctor Traut arrived, everyone, including Doctor Traut, stood when she came in. Once, later on, while I was assisting her in surgery, I said, "You do that exactly like Doctor Morton" (who was our idol). She replied, "It should be; I taught him." In 1954, she was honored as the outstanding woman doctor in the country when she received the Elizabeth Blackwell Award in New York City. She was the only woman to hold the office of president of the Pacific Coast Society of Obstetrics and Gynecology. She was the only woman, at that time, to be elected to the board of governors of The American College of Surgeons. She was chairman of the obstetrics and gynecology section of the American Medical Association. She belonged to all the most prestigious societies. She continued to practice for a number of years, but we were sad to see such a wonderful woman leave our institution.

A number of the faculty and residents who worked in Doctor Traut's department became chairman of other departments: Moore became chairman at Columbia and later at UCLA. Merrill became chairman at Oklahoma. When Doctor Traut gave up being chairman,

Doctor Morton, being passed over for that position for Ernest Page, moved to be chairman at UCLA. Both Morton and Moore became presidents of The American Board of Obstetrics and Gynecology. Unfortunately, Traut was not able to get any of his well-trained people to stay on to succeed him. Being uncertain of their future at UCSF, good men left for appointments elsewhere.

Doctor Traut did not want his residents to be married. He felt that it would take time away from their duties at the hospital. He was able to prevail with that point of view quite well until the war. When we came back from the war, it was more difficult to dictate a matter such as marriage to us. Our feeling was, "Give us a job to do, and we will do it." Reprimand us if we do not do our work adequately. But please do not tell us how to live our private lives. The professor saw the light and learned to accept a practice of which he did not approve.

After my training at UC Hospital in pathology and as a teaching assistant to Doctor Traut, I was assigned to St. Luke's Hospital—first as assistant resident, then as chief resident. On my last night on call at UC, a patient came in with what I was sure was a ruptured tubal pregnancy. She was a private patient of one of our best faculty members, Earl King. I confirmed my impression by inserting a needle into the woman's peritoneal cavity through the vagina and withdrawing blood that did not clot. That meant the blood had not been obtained from putting the needle in a blood vessel; rather, the blood was free in the abdominal cavity, mixed with peritoneal fluid of the abdomen. I called Doctor King and told him I was crossmatching blood, but that the woman was obviously losing a great deal internally. He said that I should take her to surgery immediately, prepare to transfuse her with her own blood from the peritoneal cavity (which we did at that time), and get started. He would be right there, as he lived only a couple of blocks from the hospital. I did as he ordered. The patient was in the operating room ready for surgery, an anesthetic had been started, and blood was running, but it seemed that the patient was losing more than we were giving her. At that point my surgery experience was still limited. Most of my training has been in obstetrics. I thought I had better get started, counting on Doctor King being present. I opened the patient's abdomen and found a great deal of blood, as well as a major rupture of a fallopian tube with the pregnancy extruding. I removed the tube, and bleeding stopped. Blood was pumped from the patient's abdomen, filtered through gauze, and transfused back into her. She was doing much better, but still no Doctor King. I closed the patient's abdomen and sent her to recovery in good shape. I was upset, wondering if I had done the right thing. I called Doctor King's home only to get a busy signal. A few hours later, as the new day began, I got a call from Doctor King, asking if I had called him during the night. I told him the whole story. He said he had awakened with the phone near his bed off the hook. He came by to see the patient to say that all had gone as planned, or words to that effect. The patient seemed happy. Interestingly, those were the days before anxiety about malpractice suits.

St. Luke's Hospital was entirely different from the university hospital. It had a staff of mostly good gynecologists. They had a small clinic. But the big difference for us in training was that we were treated with great respect and consideration. We got the best quarters and the best food—even better than the attending physicians. We ate meals not in house staff quarters, but at the same "horseshoe table" with the attendings. Further, the attendings had us do most of their surgery, under their supervision. That sort of thing occurred in the university hospital rarely, except with chief residents. We learned a good deal more than we had expected of a private hospital.

There was one horrible experience I cannot forget. A young woman was in labor with her first baby. She was being cared for by a doctor for whom I had had respect. Labor stopped progressing, with the baby too high to apply forceps. The doctor elected to do a version and extraction, which meant that he would push the baby back into the uterus, turn it so that it was feet first, and deliver it with traction on the feet, as well as other maneuvers. This procedure required both deep anesthesia to relax the uterus, and that there not be too large a baby. The danger was tearing the uterus. The anesthesiologist did his best. The turning of the baby and the extraction were difficult. The baby died shortly after birth. The mother began to bleed profusely. All maneuvers to control the bleeding failed. The doctor exited the room, leaving me in charge. I tried to transfuse the mother, but I could not get ahead of the hemorrhage. Obviously, the uterus had ruptured. The mother died. To this day, I cannot forget this horror—the only maternal death I had ever witnessed. I cannot forget that doctor's action. The only thing that could have saved this woman was immediate surgery, probably in the same room, which was equipped only for delivery. That was the only version and extraction I had ever seen attempted, except for a second twin. Obviously a cesarean section would have avoided all of this. I never had the courage to ask the doctor how many versions he had done. I was only a second-year resident. Years later, as a consultant, I was able to save a patient who had a similar rupture following a difficult breech delivery. I had learned from this earlier tragedy.

From St. Luke's, I went back to San Francisco County Hospital as chief resident. I set myself up in elegant quarters, which had been part of the newest of the buildings that made up the County. I had a large room with a double bed, a complete bathroom, and plenty of windows. When I was on call, which was often, Gwen would come to stay. We got meals in the cafeteria. I learned how to be an administrator and a teacher. There was plenty to do.

When my term at the County was up, I returned to the UC Hospital for an additional six months. It was time to think of the future. There was one junior faculty appointment available; the choice was between J.G. Moore and me. Moore was chosen. That meant that my best choice was to go into private practice, since I did not want to go elsewhere for a faculty position. San Francisco was my home.

I got some good advice from Doctor Traut. At the time, it was the practice of doctors in our profession to ask patients who were to have a baby or an operation how much their husbands made, and to charge accordingly. Doctor Traut found that practice abhorrent. He said he wanted me to charge all patients the same for the same service. I would have the leeway of lowering charges for those in need. He said that well-off patients would often ask why I had not charged as much as their friends had been charged. He said that I should say that I had a fund to which that patient could give if she desired. The money would be used for teaching and research in my specialty. That bit of advice had a profound effect on my life. I did not become wealthy, but my fund has grown steadily.

I always felt that Doctor Traut was one of the best teachers I had met in my medical career. I had hoped to continue in academic medicine; however, Doctor Traut chose Gerry Moore over me. I thought he could have found me a spot. When Gerry left to join Doctor Morton at U.C.L.A., Doctor Traut called and offered me a position on his staff. At that point, I had been in practice for a year or so and had invested time and money. I thanked him for the offer but refused. I found that I was enjoying being my own boss. So, in a way, Doctor Traut had done me a favor by sending me into private practice. Interestingly, in the last days of his illness, he often invited me to reminisce. I always thought his biggest mistake in life was in not keeping his best men around him for support. When he became ill, he did not have a staff organized to take over for him. That left an opening for Doctor Page, who was anxious to take on the job of chief. Doctor Page was a superb lecturer on scientific subjects and had impressed a national meeting. He also had published a large number of articles in scientific journals. Though he had not been on the academic faculty, he was able to convince the powers that he should be selected as chairman.

Chapter 3

Private Practice, 1949

In 1949, a large number of doctors were getting ready to go into private practice. Some had been slow to get released from the armed services; some, like me, had finished postgraduate training, and having seen San Francisco during our military duty, wanted to settle there. That made finding suitable office space very difficult and expensive. A number of buildings had been converted from residential to professional. In those buildings, it was the responsibility of the new tenant to convert his area from residential to a medical office. That, of course, was more expensive downtown than farther out. Historically, in San Francisco, the most prestigious office buildings for medical professionals were near the center of the city—384 Post on Union Square was considered the best, and 490 Post, a block away, was almost as good. The newer 450 Sutter was all right, but not quite as classy. The converted buildings were considered a step down. Space was difficult to find. There was a very nice building on Van Ness Avenue and Jackson. It was much more accessible, and it had some well-known occupants. It was halfway between downtown and most hospitals. It was full. My best friend Ernie Rogers and I moved into a building a block north at 2107 Van Ness. It was being converted, and the rent was more reasonable. Also, the modification was within my meager budget. It soon was filled with well-qualified doctors who were starting out: Kurt Newgard, a refugee who received postgraduate training in Chicago; Joe Presti, a well-trained young urologist; and Alan Palmer, a brilliant man who had been a UCSF faculty member in gynecology, with a special interest in infertility. Maurice Robinson had an excellent radiology office, and he helped Palmer and me with our work. He was recognized as one of the best in the city. There was also a superb psychoanalyst, Fred Alston. So Ernie and I had good company.

We opened our offices. My mother was a world-class decorator, so my waiting room was lovely, with French provincial furniture. It was not so practical, but inviting. I sent out the usual announcements, and, at the suggestion of friends, hired a lovely young Irish woman, Pauline O'Dougherty, as a secretary. The response to my announcements was minimal. There was a drugstore on the first floor of our building, and it had a counter where one could get simple food. I had tea most afternoons with Ern.

Among my first patients were a group of San Francisco Giants players' wives. Felipe Alou's wife and Annie Cepeda I remember particularly. Felipe's wife was pregnant. One day, he brought her to the office. He was a big man. He sat in one of those lovely French Provincial chairs, and it exploded. The arms came off, and the back went backward. He was devastated. I made light of the situation. Fortunately, my mother had a good man to repair the damage. I added a couple of more substantial chairs to my waiting room. This was one of many lessons that I learned early on in practice.

Shortly after I started practice, Doctor Traut called me to his office. He said, "John, don't you think that it would be a good idea if a society of former residents in our department was formed?" I agreed. He then said, "I hope you will volunteer to form the organization." I of course said, "Yes Sir." So, I got a list of all the former residents and sent invitations to a meeting to be held in one of the nice small dinning rooms of The Fairmont Hotel. I got an estimated price per head and included that in the invitation. The evening was a big success, though Doctor Traut did not come because he was not a former resident. Phil Arnot made a perfect leader. He had been one of the first residents and was a good storyteller. Further, he was good at remembering names. There was an "open bar." I thought that the guests would have a drink, or at the most two. When I got the bill, I found that I was out about two hundred dollars, which was a lot in those days. Obviously, this was a good drinking bunch. I learned a good lesson. The society continued to grow and the annual meeting was held at the time of some major meetings in San Francisco. This encouraged former residents who lived far away to come not only for our gathering, but also for the meeting. I always provided a guest speaker who would speak on an entertaining subject. After a couple of meetings, Sid Gospe, a former resident, suggested that we name the society FROG for Former Residents in Obstetrics and Gynecology. The idea was accepted immediately. The wife of one of the residents designed a small frog pin. We each got one, and it became our custom to give one to each of the new members. I was the president for a number of years, but finally got others to take on the job. Strangely, after about thirty years, the FROG Society faded away. That was mostly due to the fact that more and more of the residents are women. They were reluctant to give up a night with their families. I hope that I can resurrect the society. We had fine times, and residents at UCSF have been like a family. If the society is activated again, I will be sure that there will be a bar, but it will not be "open."

My first patients came from sisters at St. Mary's Hospital, where I had spent six months in training, and from faculty members at UC, particularly Leon Goldman, who was professor of surgery. Because I am Jewish, I had expected that the many Jewish doctors I knew would be a major source of patients. They sent their wives, but no patients. They wanted to send patients to doctors who would refer to them, and I, starting out, had little opportunity to refer. I tried to explore all sorts of areas that might enhance my practice. I went to lunch at St. Luke's, where I had worked as a resident and knew a number of men. They often asked me for "curbside" consultations, but rarely sent a patient. I tried the Franklin Hospital, where I was welcome, but again, few patients. I did have entree to all the hospitals, because I now was one of the best-trained young doctors in my specialty in San Francisco.

My experience at Mount Zion Hospital was strange. I went to talk to Franklin Harris, who was Chief of Staff and had great influence. He said that he would love to have me at Mount Zion, but he wanted me to do only obstetrics and no surgery. (He and other surgeons at Mount Zion had been doing all the gynecological surgery—often with poor indications.) I said that I had spent years of training in gynecological surgery, and if I could not do that, I was not interested in Mount Zion. He backed down and said, in my case, he would permit me to do surgery.

Gradually, as my contemporaries got established, I was sent more patients, and satisfied patients sent their friends. Because I was a veteran, I received a monthly stipend of about $125 for six months. This was to be stopped when my income exceeded $500. That stipend, combined with some help from my family, got me started.

Doctor Traut asked me to start an infertility clinic at UC. In addition to expanding my use of hysterosalpingograms, which could show abnormal canals in the uterus or tubes, I designed an instrument with which I could recover mucus from the canal into the uterus after intercourse. There I could count the number of sperm present and assess their motility and structure. I could also evaluate the chemical qualities of the mucus. By treating abnormalities, I began to find that heretofore infertile patients were conceiving. I tried to correct damaged fallopian tubes using magnification, but I canceled that. My success rate did not justify the complicated surgery. However, I did learn to use various instruments to magnify the surgical areas. Later, a group of infertility experts devised ways to bypass blocked tubes; by that time, I felt that should not be my main area of interest, and I left infertility to those who wished to devote their entire practice to that problem. I did find, though, that helping infertile women to conceive was rewarding.

A senior obstetrician at Mount Zion asked me to see a patient of his for whom he had just delivered a breech baby. I went to see her, and she appeared to have a ruptured uterus (a major emergency). I told him that I thought he should get blood crossmatched and take her to surgery at once. I would be glad to help him. He decided to wait until a friend of his came in the following morning. I told the laboratory to crossmatch four units of blood. By the time the obstetrician's friend arrived hours later, the patient was in desperate condition. She was taken to surgery, where I was asked to help. The anesthesiologist was having a terrible time trying to keep the patient out of shock by pumping in blood and even giving an arterial transfusion, which is rare. The patient did have a ruptured uterus, with huge blood loss. We were able to stop the bleeding and do proper surgery, which was difficult because of the swelling associated with the rupture. The patient survived. I think I got an assistant's fee of fifty dollars. More important, I began to be treated with more respect.

At this point, the war in Korea started, and there was a question as to whether I would have to go. After World War II, doctors were never given discharge certificates. They were on inactive reserve. I had two small children, and had invested in getting a practice started. Fortunately, I had just enough time in service to keep me from having to go, whereas some of my friends had to give up their practice and return to military duty. Interestingly, fifty years later I found that I had received another decoration just prior to my discharge. Had that decoration been recorded earlier, I would have had five additional points, which probably would have resulted in my being relieved of duty earlier. Had that happened, I would have not had enough time in service, and would have had to go to Korea.

At this time, doctors of my generation began to appear on the scene in greater numbers. Leonard Rosenman was a well-trained general surgeon from the Harvard program. He and I had been trained to review all surgery. This had not been done in any of the hospitals in San Francisco outside of the university ones. Quality control had been left to the various chiefs. We pushed for and got a tissue committee. This committee was to review all surgery. Laboratory reports on tissue removed were reviewed; the committee was to decide whether the surgery had been indicated, and if the proper operation had been done. It soon became evident that the surgery performed by some of our senior surgeons was questioned. When that happened, the tissue committee meetings began to get more attendance than any others. The largest conference room was filled. Doctors on the staff were amazed to see that the tissue committee was willing to question the nature of the surgery performed by the chief of staff and other senior surgeons. The result was remarkable! There was a rapid drop in questionable operations, and some surgeons even took surgery to other hospitals to avoid review of their indications and procedures. A common question that was brought up was whether, in doing a hysterectomy, the uterine cervix was left. Hysterectomy was much easier if the cervix was left in place, but a greater potential for cervical cancer was also risked. At the time, cervical smears were just beginning to be done. So, it was uncertain in many operations as to whether a potential cancer was left behind. There were also questions as to whether the ovaries should be left when they were a potential source of cancer, but also a source of hormones, which we were just learning to replace. So, young doctors on the staff of Mount Zion had a great effect on the quality of surgery performed, even by expert surgeons. One could be an expert surgeon, but operate with poor indication and do the wrong procedure.

The new young, well-trained doctors were often the products of excellent resident training programs, so it was natural for them to be interested in establishing training programs in their hospitals. Though small, by the 1950s Mount Zion Hospital was the home of superior training programs in medicine and surgery, and I was pushing for programs in obstetrics and gynecology, as well as pediatrics.

There was a great deal of resistance by the general surgeons to the concept of a department of obstetrics and gynecology. They did not mind a department of obstetrics, but they did not want to relinquish a major source of income represented by gynecological surgery. Most of the general surgeons had little or no training in vaginal surgery, which was mostly in the repair of injuries of vaginal childbirth, but they performed it, often poorly. They could only do adequate abdominal surgery. Gradually, over the years, the operating room required that surgeons have approval for the surgery they wanted to perform. The quality of care steadily improved.

Finally, after a few years of demonstrating that there was a place for the gynecological surgeon, we convinced the chief of staff, Franklin I. Harris, that there should be a department of obstetrics and gynecology. The first chief, Harry Jurow, tried to establish a training program, but he did not have the time to get it organized, and he did not get the full support of his colleagues. In 1966, I was appointed chief.

1949 to 1966 was a time for me to mature as a member of the professional community and as a practitioner of obstetrics and gynecology.

My second son Jim was born on February 5, 1956. Gwen began labor, and I was ready to take her to the hospital when our older son became very ill with a high fever. Gwen said, "I can't leave Johnny!" and her labor stopped. The next morning his fever broke, and her labor resumed. There is no question that I learned a good deal of obstetrics from Gwen's pregnancies.

Chapter 4

Helen Rowan

Certain of my patients had a profound effect on me and my life as a doctor. One of the first was Helen Rowan.

Before she came to San Francisco, Helen had gone to Mills College, The State Department, and then The Carnegie Corporation. She was referred to me by Julius Krevans, who at the time was a professor of medicine at UCSF. Helen had no major gynecological problem when I first saw her. Early on, she impressed me as being an unusual woman. I liked her enthusiasm, her sensitivity, her honesty, and her sense of humor. She had an aliveness that was refreshing in an otherwise busy day. She was a crusader who could be furious at the injustices of the world, and shared my hatred of the abortion situation in our country. She had written a highly important article on the discrimination and injustices suffered by Mexican Americans in the United States.

I had not seen Helen for a while because she was young, and I thought that visiting my office twice a year was adequate. During one of those intervals, she developed pelvic symptoms. I was on my first trip to Europe, so my new partner Alan Margolis saw her and noted an abnormality in her pelvis. He looked though my notes and found that this was a new finding, and he advised that she should have surgery to determine the nature of this mass. At the time, there was no ultrasound, no CT, and no MRI. X-rays were of minimal value. Helen decided that she would like to postpone any surgery until I returned from Europe.

When I checked in at my office, one of the first things that Alan told me was that there was some sort of a mass in Helen's pelvis. I got her in at once and, of course, noted the change in her pelvic examination. With her approval, I scheduled surgery after suitable workup. She had a wild ovarian cancer. Though its total mass was not great, it involved all of the neighboring organs. I did an extensive operation, removing all visible tumor, the uterus, both tubes and ovaries, and the omentum (a large fatty pad in the abdomen, a frequent place for cancer to spread). She was then treated with irradiation and chemotherapy under the best available supervision. Sadly the tumor recurred a few months later. Now, I learned what a wonderful woman she was, and I learned a great deal about relationships with patients.

She amazed me. She treated her cancer not as a bitter, unjust blow of fate, but merely as a monumental inconvenience. I got in the habit of stopping by her apartment on my way home from my office, even though there was little I could do. I think she was looking after me. She had a serenity, a strength, a balance, and wisdom that to that point in my life were unmatched. Here was a person who could be furious at the injustices of the world, but did not view her prolonged illness as unjust. The physically debilitating effects of her cancer and its treatment did not manifest themselves in anger, fear, or self-pity.

With all of her problems, she continued to live an active, involved life. She often had friends visiting when I stopped by. She got out and explored San Francisco. She had a special love affair with the sights, sounds, and smells of the city. She would go out to dinner with friends, though often she could eat very little. She never lost her sense of humor, particularly when amused at herself. She had comments about hospital gowns and the paperwork involved in getting treated. She often poked fun at the attitudes, the words, or the deeds of a particularly pretentious, condescending, or arrogant politician, bureaucrat, doctor, or other public figure.

I was amazed at the numbers of important people that assembled at her apartment, and later at her bedside. People like John Gardner, her former boss, traveled regularly from Washington to visit with her. Julius Krevans, who became dean and then chancellor at UCSF, found time to visit with her. There was no great solemnity. They asked her opinions. They talked about their problems. She was a great listener. She paid attention. Soon, I began telling her about my problems with patients or in-office management. Somehow, she was able to make me smile.

Even in her illness, she was generous in her friendships—almost to a fault. One day, I found that a son of a friend had put his sleeping bag in the corner of her living room for a while. I know that she put up bail for a young friend who got picked up for throwing a joint out of his car in the presence of local police. She took a great interest in me and my professional efforts, and encouraged me to keep on working with cancer. She was sure that I would find ways to improve cure rates.

When she died two years after surgery, she left a letter for me. In it, she thanked me for my care and friendship, and she insisted that I not feel guilty for not having cured her. She set up a fund in my name; it contained $5,000, which was a significant sum at that time. It was to be known as the JOHN A. KERNER FOUNDATION. To quote the document: "a) The purpose of the Foundation shall be to advance the practice of medicine in the field of obstetrics and gynecology, as well as to establish teaching funds for fellows and students in that field. b) The foregoing enumeration purposes shall not be construed as a limitation upon the use of the funds of the Foundation by Dr. Kerner, but he shall in his sole discretion, expend the funds for any purpose in the field of obstetrics and gynecology."

That gift and that document changed my life. I never earned huge sums of money, in part because I gave a good deal of pro bono time to the university and to teaching at Mount Zion. My various partners sometimes objected to that. Patients heard of my fund and began to give generously to it. Now, at the later part of my life, I find that the fund started by Helen has provided over $4 million to various projects, originally in teaching, but recently more in cancer. Helen's donation fit in with the plan that was suggested by Doctor Traut. At this point, my interest in cancer diagnosis and treatment got a major stimulus. I hoped that I could learn to protect women from the terrible disease that Helen had, but if they got it, I hoped to help develop a cure.

She also left me a beautiful, carved wooden head that she had obtained in Africa when she worked for the Carnegie Corporation. It is in a prominent place in my home, and when I see it I think of her.

John Gardner told me a story about her and her candor. He was interviewing her for a job at the Carnegie Corporation. After carefully reviewing her application, he noted the unusual number of prior employers. He asked: "Would you say you are a restless person, Miss Rowan?" Her answer was immediate and to the point: "I am restless, but not irresponsible." She was hired on the spot.

There was a Greek of old who noted that we can't be sure of a man's character and education until we know how he dies. She taught me about this, and how to relate to the dying. She also started me on the long journey to find a cure for cancer.

Chapter 5

Maturing, the 50's

As I became more and more established, I had three major interests: my growing family, teaching, and honing my professional skills, especially in the field of cancer. I had three children—two boys, and then a girl, Jan, born June 15, 1956. I spent a good deal of time at The University of California Clinic, where, encouraged by my neighbor, Alan Palmer, I had a special interest in infertility. I also was involved in the teaching of any residents we had at Mount Zion. I became less involved with other hospitals except Children's, since by now most of my patients were referred from Mount Zion, and a few from the university.

My practice at first was mostly obstetrics. It was my habit to go to the hospital to meet my patients when they were admitted in labor. That was unusual, since most obstetricians had their patients evaluated by staff, and then decided on what to do after a phone consultation. My procedure was reassuring for the patients. Because of this, Gwen insisted that we live near Mount Zion and Children's hospitals, so that I could get home faster to see her and my children. That proved to be very important for our quality of life. We bought a home with the profit from the sale of our apartment, and with some help from my parents. It was perfectly located between Mount Zion and Children's hospitals.

The value of my way was illustrated by a case. A lawyer's wife was pregnant with her third child. She was at term. She called me at home to say that she thought she was in labor. I told her it would be best if I checked her, and asked her to come to the emergency room of Mount Zion. When she arrived, I was there waiting for her. She was having mild contractions, her bag of waters had ruptured while she was en route. I checked her and she was well. The baby's heart was acting a little strangely. I did a pelvic examination and found the baby presenting as a breech, but the cord had prolapsed into the vagina. The prolapse resulted in compression of the cord whenever there was a contraction. The baby was very large. I pushed the breech up and kept it from compressing the cord. I got on the gurney with the patient and asked for immediate surgery and blood to be crossmatched. We got to surgery with me still holding the baby back, which was not easy. The contractions were getting stronger. When the patient was ready for surgery, I instructed a nurse on how to hold the baby back, then I rapidly prepared myself. The patient was given a rapid anesthetic, and I delivered a nine-pound, ten-ounce baby. The baby was fine. My habit of being there paid off. The baby is now a lawyer in his father's old firm.

Young specialists must pass the American Board in their specialty. Until World War II, there were not many board-qualified specialists, but the young doctors returning from the service had become aware of their value. They had noted that board-qualified men got better jobs and more pay. There were four basic steps to get the boards. You had to complete a residency of at least three years, which included achieving the rank of head resident. You had to be in practice for at least two years. You had to have done and documented a minimum number of deliveries and operations (for physicians specializing in obstetrics and gynecology). Finally, you had to take the The American Board examination. At that time, the examination was given in New York. I was confident because of my training, but I knew other well-trained men had failed. The examination had three basic parts: microscope slides pathology, gross pathology, and oral. Doctor Morton, who had been an examiner, had coached me. He said if the question was controversial, I should answer what I had been taught. The format for the microscopic was that you were given a number of difficult slides to identify. If you missed any, you were given a second set, the size of which was dependent on the number missed. I was good at pathology, especially because of my interest in cancer, and got my first set right in short order. I then moved on to gross pathology, presented to me by a doctor who knew my professor. I was able to identify and discuss anything he gave me. Finally, the oral was given by two men. They took turns asking questions. If I seemed to know the answer, they would stop me and go to something else. I was prepared for that format and did well. Though the examination was scheduled to take two days, at the end of the first day, the secretary said I did not have to return. I did not understand. She said that I shouldn't worry. If they did not ask me back, I was in. I had told Gwen that I would meet her in the King Cole Bar of the St. Regis in the late afternoon. We were ecstatic. I had passed in record time. We had a free day in New York. We had been fortunate to get tickets to a show that had just opened, "Guys and Dolls." It was spectacular. I loved every minute. It was a great day.

Having passed the Board, it was easy to become a member of The American College of Surgeons after a brief examination, and also The American College of Obstetricians and Gynecologists. These were important should I wish to progress in academic medicine.

Now, with my qualifications, I was called upon to give talks at medical societies around the state. Some of these talks were sponsored by the American Cancer Society, and some were the result of requests to my department at UC. I did not have an easy time. My main goal was to sell the Papanicolaou-Traut vaginal smear for diagnosis of uterine cancer. I continued to get a great deal of opposition from pathologists who insisted that a diagnosis could not be made without tissue. As noted before, it took me a long time to convince them that the smear would alert to early cancer, even to precancerous lesions. Doctor Traut, with some help from me, began to convince pathologists, especially the Chief at UCSF. I was paid very little for these lectures, often no more than a dinner. Occasionally Gwen would go along.

As I had mentioned, Alan Palmer was in the building on Van Ness Avenue. He was in many ways a genius. He designed and patented the recessed door handles used on most modern cars to replace the old ones that projected out. During World War II, he designed the first modern flak jackets after studying the wounds sustained by English pilots in the Battle for Britain. He also was on the board that decided where bombing would be most effective. He was the first to relate basal body temperature to ovulation. The basal temperature is taken the first thing in the morning, before getting out of bed. It rises and stays elevated after ovulation until a period begins, then it drops. It remains elevated in pregnancy. He was interested in infertility, and I learned a great deal from him. Doctor Traut fired him from the faculty because of his erratic nature and tendency to drink too much. From Alan I learned how to evaluate an infertile woman and how to apply that knowledge toward correcting the problem. I then was able to supervise a successful infertility clinic at UCSF. This was the first major clinic of that sort in San Francisco. It was also a good place for me to teach UC residents.

There was a test for determining whether the fallopian tubes were blocked, the Ruben's Test. It consisted of blowing gas through the uterine cervix and observing its passage through the tubes. That was indicated by listening to the abdomen with a stethoscope for the special sound, and also by noting the appearance of shoulder pain caused by the gas collecting under the diaphragm. Alan had me get a machine that showed the contractions of the tubes in the presence of the gas, and it also showed the drop in pressure when the gas went through. There was also a tracing of the gas pressure. When the tubal pattern was not clear, or when gas did not go through the tube, the problem was: What caused the abnormality? Alan and I ran the first major series of hysterosalpingograms (a study of the inside of the uterus and tubes) using a radiopaque medium, Lipiodol Ultra Fluid, which he got from France. The agents used at that time were absorbed rapidly and did not give adequate information, particularly in relation to tubal patency. We would get a film in twenty-four hours. If the medium was present in a diffuse way in the abdomen, we could be sure that at least one tube was patent, though we usually got a clear picture of the inside of the uterus and tubes. So a blockage of the passages could be seen. That was extremely valuable in infertility studies. It let us know which area we should try to correct. If the material was collected around the ends of the tubes, we could be quite sure of either blocked tubes or scarring in the area. With the water-soluble agents, the rapid absorption prevented the twenty-four hour films from being of much value. We never had problems with the Ethiodol. In those days there was not a major malpractice problem, nor was there much done to control new agents. We never asked for permission from anyone to try the new agent. We each got proper instruments from France, and the instrument maker at UCSF made excellent cannulas, which I used to introduce the radiopaque material. Those cannulas were held in place by literally screwing them into the uterine cervix. This was easier than holding the cannulas in place with a tenaculum (a long, toothed instrument), and it was less painful. These instruments did traumatize the lining of the cervix. In 1953, Alan devised a cannula held on by suction, and now, over fifty years later, that is the technique most widely used. An unexpected dividend of just doing the hysterosalpingogram was fairly often a pregnancy. We believed that the procedure could force dried-out mucus out of the tube, thus clearing it for the passage of an egg.

After doing a thousand of these procedures, we decided to make moving pictures using image intensifiers and X-rays. The films were marvelous for teaching, and I was invited to present that work at the Third World Congress on Fertility and Sterility in Amsterdam on June 7, 1959. However, we stopped doing the movies because we worried about the possible danger of excessive irradiation. Unfortunately, at this point, Alan died in a home accident.

I continued the work. My papers on these techniques were the first published, and the technique came to be widely used. Interestingly, many years later, a paper was published in a major journal which gave the same information that I had provided. The author of that paper did not give me or Alan credit. Perhaps he did not check the literature thoroughly.

Gwen and I made our first trip to Europe in 1958. It was a great experience for us to visit London, Paris, Venice, Florence, and Rome. On that trip we met the man whose company was manufacturing the Lipiodol Ultra Fluid that I was using for the hysterograms. He wanted the material to be used regularly in the United States. In large part because of the work done by Alan Palmer and me, he could demonstrate that his product caused no major problems. The material was released in the United States as Lipiodol.

At that time, I was called upon to lecture mostly on infertility, and I became skilled at procedures that might improve fertility. I found that the most meticulous surgery was not effective often enough to be justified. I could repair many defects of the uterus with success, but even using a dissecting microscope in surgery, my success rate in opening blocked tubes and making them function was low. A careful workup, including tubal studies, various endocrine techniques, and patient education, were quite effective. Though we tried it often, artificial insemination was not as successful then as it is now.

The fund established by Helen Rowan grew steadily as I followed the advice of Doctor Traut in keeping my fees uniform while encouraging gifts to the fund if the patient or family wished. At first, The Kerner Foundation funds were used mostly to enhance teaching of residents at Mount Zion. There never had been enough money to provide a first-rate program. Now, as funds increased, it became possible to set up an excellent library, to send residents to national meetings, and often to provide financial support for residents. Also, I could reimburse certain teachers. Later on, the foundation became much more concerned with cancer research. In 1974, the Kerner Fund established a cancer research program at Mount Zion under the leadership of Ira Goldfine, using the new concepts of molecular biology. The work there was a factor in developing a major cancer center at Mount Zion when UCSF and Mount Zion merged in 1990.

Shortly after the war, colleagues and I felt that we should have a residency program at Mount Zion. Few private hospitals had approved residency programs in obstetrics and gynecology. Such programs required three years of specialized training approved by the American Board. At the time, I had not yet passed the board, and passage was required for a program chair. The program was started by Doctor Jurow, with help from me and others; however, it just did not take off. It did not provide the material or the supervision that the Board required, and it did not receive formal approval. Doctor Jurow lived out of San Francisco, but he did try. It just was not enough. In the face of the problems, he resigned his position. He needed more-well trained people as teachers, and a greater number of patients. Now, having passed the board, I was asked to take over after a vote by the Medical Board and the Mount Zion Hospital Board of Directors.

I had a challenge. I felt that I needed the kind of help one can get only from a young doctor who had gone through a good residency program. Also, I needed help in my growing practice. My personal physician warned that if I did not get help, I would not be around long. Alan Margolis was known to me when he was a resident at UCSF, and he had been a friend of my brother in college. He was an outstanding resident. After his residency, he did service in the Army, as was then required. He agreed to work with me as long as he could continue his research at UC. He was a wonderful partner in my office, and a superb teacher. My program got unequivocal approval by The American Board of Obstetrics and Gynecology, and we began to get excellent candidates for our program. Alan and I felt that our graduating residents were better surgeons than those at UC.

With Alan as a partner, our practice began to grow rapidly. We decided that it would be wise to move closer to Mount Zion. That was a radical move at that time, since most doctors were still looking for prestige locations downtown. My good friend Alan Abrams, who was an excellent internist, had a father-in-law with good imagination, Fred Zelinsky. Fred bought an old, horseshoe-shaped apartment building across from Mount Zion, and converted it to offices, the general design of which was left to the new tenants.

I worked out a plan for offices larger than we had on Van Ness. We would have three examining rooms, two consultation rooms, a large business area, and a waiting room. We were required to do the detail work. I had always been quite good at woodworking since grammar school wood shop, so I made some of the cabinets, the writing desks in the examining rooms, containers for charts to place on the door of each examining room, and a drying rack for rubber gloves. (We did not have disposable gloves at that time.) All of this carpentry was made possible because our friend, Morton Weinstein, had a wonderful workshop in the basement of his new home. Having settled on the design for a desk that could be fastened to the wall, I found it easy to make three— one for each room. Of course, the same procedure was used for the chart containers. I was proud of the work, and enjoyed the fact that I had saved a good deal of money. Since I did the work in the evening after working all day, I was fortunate that I had no accidents using the power tools.

The move proved to be wonderful for me. It was much easier to do good obstetrics, because I only had to cross the street to the hospital for surgery or for the obstetrical department. Also, our building had a superb group of physicians: Alan Abrams; Don Bernstein, a fine internist; Harris Fishbon, a senior superb teacher of internal medicine; Bud Solomon, a top eye doctor; and a number more. As time went by, Don had to retire early, and Bud needed more space elsewhere, which made it possible to enlarge my office. With the support of my well-qualified neighbors and colleagues, I now became a major player at Mount Zion, and to a degree at The University of California, San Francisco.

Chapter 6

Alan Margolis

Alan Margolis was a credit to our profession. He was a favorite teacher, both at Mount Zion and at UCSF. He was interested not only in being a good practitioner, but also in advancing the cause of women and improving our knowledge of pregnancy. These talents eventually led to his becoming full-time on the university faculty.

He was interested in the physiology of the placenta, and he tried valiantly to keep placentas alive after they were delivered. He had limited success, but no one before him had done as well. Then he transferred our major interest to erythroblastosis fetalis.

Erythroblastosis is a disease that has been known for generations, but it was not understood until the 1940s. When I was in training, what we knew about blood at first was that there were four types: A,B, AB, and O. But in our attempts to crossmatch blood, at times we found matches that we expected to work did not. At that point, hematologists thought there must be some subgroups. At UCSF, the hematologists under Stacy Mettier discovered the Rh blood factor. They found that some people's blood contained that factor, and some did not. In obstetrics, it was noted that the condition erythroblastosis fetalis was associated with anemia, which in turn led to swelling of tissues and other complications, usually ending in fetal death. Doctors knew that erythroblastosis rarely occurred in firstborns, but was more common in second babies, and usually much worse in third pregnancies. Finally, it was postulated that the cause of erythroblastosis was related to a Rh-negative mother with an Rh-positive baby. In pregnancy, if the baby is RH-positive, as small amount of the baby's blood crosses the placenta into the mother's circulation, the mother becomes allergic to Rh-positive. That being so, with a second pregnancy, if the baby is Rh positive, the mother will begin to destroy the red blood cells of the fetus.

This problem was dealt with by measuring how strong the mother's reaction to the baby's blood was, and if the reaction seemed to be severe, and if the baby were close to term, labor would be induced, and the baby would be delivered, then transfused with Rh-negative blood; this was done by using the vessels from the umbilical cord. The problem with this was that the measure of severity of involvement by doing blood titers was far from accurate, and babies were often delivered before it was necessary, or too late.

At this point a doctor in England made a suggestion that if we studied the amniotic fluid by studying its optical density, we might be more accurate. This line of reasoning was associated with noting that at delivery of erythroblastotic infants, the amniotic fluid was always discolored by breakdown products of blood produced by the mother's antibodies destroying the baby's blood. The idea was picked up by Doctor Lilly in New Zealand. He collected amniotic fluid by inserting a needle through the abdominal wall into the amniotic sac. He then studied the fluid to determine the optical density of the fraction that related to blood breakdown. He created a curve from which risk could be determined, and therefore a much more accurate way for determining risk of prolonging pregnancy in the presence of erythroblastosis was possible.

An attempt to duplicate Lilly's work failed at an institution in Southern California. Alan Margolis suggested that he and I try to reproduce the technique. Neither of us had ever seen the procedure done, nor did we know anyone who had done it. We knew there were risks of doing damage with the needle, of infection, of causing labor, or other complication. On the other hand, malpractice problems were not a major worry in those days. So we started. We proceeded with extreme care in getting the first specimens. We decided where it would be the most safe to place the needles. When we took our fluid to our lab, at first the readings of the optical density did not seem to relate to those of Doctor Lilly. Finally, a chemist in our laboratory figured out how the fluid should be studied to conform with the information from New Zealand. We had done it.

After doing a few cases, we realized that we had in our hands a valuable tool. The University of California could not duplicate our finding, so, for some months they sent their amniotic fluid specimens to our lab for evaluation.

Now, we knew when the best time to deliver babies with erythroblastosis was. However, the time was often so early in pregnancy that the baby could not survive, even with exchange transfusion.

So again Doctor Lilly came up with a suggestion. We should transfuse the baby in the mother's uterus. How to do that? Put a needle through the abdominal wall into the abdomen of the baby, and then pass Rh-negative blood through the needle—ideally by passing a catheter through the needle into the baby's abdominal cavity. It was hoped that the blood would be absorbed from the abdomen and counteract the anemia of the baby long enough for it to get to term, or close to term, when it would be safer to deliver it.

Alan and I heard about this technique, but no one in the USA had tried it; so, we thought we would give it a chance. The wife of a high-ranking officer with the State of California was pregnant. She had lost a number of babies to erythroblastosis. She had been sensitized in some way prior to her first pregnancy. We decided that she would be a good candidate, and she agreed. The problem with doing this procedure was placing the needle in the right place. At that time, we did not have the use of ultrasound that we had later, so fluoroscopy with X-ray was necessary. Now, we knew that in using X-ray we would be exposing the baby and us to irradiation, so we hoped to use a minimal amount. We were able to do the procedure, and the baby lived. It proved that the technique was valid. But then we had two failures. We decided that the university had better equipment to help us in placing the needle, and we transferred the whole program there, where it did provide more infant survival.

It became obvious that we had not found the answer to the disease. My old friend and fellow intern J.G. Moore had become chief at Columbia in New York City. He and his faculty group believed that if they could inject antibodies to Rh-positive blood into pregnant mothers, those antibodies could destroy fetal blood that got into the mother's circulation before she became immunized. They got a group of Rh-negative convicts at Sing Sing in New York State to agree to be sensitized to Rh-positive. They then could inject some of the immune serum, called RhoGAM, from the convicts into the pregnant Rh-negative mother if her baby was Rh-positive. It was hoped that this would work. I was present at a faculty meeting in New York when the first findings came in. The mothers were not sensitized, so that if they were treated in the same way in future pregnancies, babies should not get erythroblastosis. Of course, they needed to do more studies to be sure.

When I arrived home, I found that my sister-in-law was pregnant. She is Rh-negative and her husband, my brother, is Rh positive. I was convinced the RhoGAM should be used. It had not been used on anyone outside of the clinical trials, but Gerry Moore agreed to send me some RhoGAM. It came in time. Though my sister-in-law's baby proved to be Rh-positive, there was no sensitization, and there were two more babies without any sign of erythroblastosis. Now the use of RhoGAM is routine in pregnancy of Rh-negative mothers, even when abortion is performed. Erythroblastosis is rare in the United States.

At this point, Alan Margolis was recruited to join the-full time faculty at UCSF. I was sad to see him go. However, I knew that UC needed him, since their teaching program was weak with the new chief, Ernest Page.

I now had a major problem. When I told my lawyer, Sam Ladar, that Alan was leaving, he asked, "How soon can he leave?" (We had a partnership agreement.) I said that his new appointment would start in about six months. Sam said, "When I said how soon can he leave, I meant it. How many hours?" I replied that I could not do that in view of the fact that Alan and I were friends, and that he had two small children. (I had delivered them.) Sam said that he could walk off with a major part of the practice that I had worked so hard to build up. Well, when Alan left, no more than a quarter of our practice followed him, but it included my wife.

I now was faced with finding someone to replace Alan. That would not be easy. I interviewed a large number of well-qualified men, and finally decided on Robert Read. He was from South Carolina and had his important training at Tulane. He proved to be a caring physician, a superb surgeon, a willing teacher, and a friend. He was ten years younger than me. Not long thereafter, we added a third doctor, Fred Berman. I had known him before he went to medical school. His mother worked for my father. (Later she worked for many years at Mount Zion.) Fred had an outstanding record at UCSF, where I got to know him when I was teaching there. I asked him to join us when Robert agreed. Fred was also an outstanding teacher and a superb surgeon, and he was wonderful with patients. The only problem I ever had with him was in the economics of practice.

With Robert, we had an agreement that he should get an increasing share of the office income until, at the end of three years, we would be equal partners. Fred felt that should not be the case with him, even though he was twenty years younger than me. We did make him a full partner in two years. Fred always felt I should get less money as I aged. That was a problem. I had absolute confidence in Robert and Fred, and never doubted their dedication and ability. I believe the feeling was mutual.

Chapter 7

Fetal Monitoring

Shortly after I became chief of Obstetrics and Gynecology at Mount Zion, I heard a great lecture by Roberto Caldeyro-Barcia of Montevideo. He had made some remarkable observations in Uruguay. He noted that fetal heart patterns provided a great deal of information about the health of the fetus, particularly in labor. I invited him to speak at our rounds at Mount Zion. I was intrigued by his observations, and thought he would be a wonderful addition to our staff, or that of UCSF. He was anxious to come, but wished to bring his staff with him. Although I could raise the money for him, his staff was beyond me, and Doctor Page at UCSF felt the same way. But I thought that we should take advantage of his observations.

Herman Uhley is an outstanding cardiologist and a friend. I consulted him as to whether he could think of some way to take advantage of the knowledge of this new observation. Herman noted that he could convert sound into signals that could be recorded, and at the same time could be sent to a nursing station. So, we strapped a receiver on the abdomens of women in labor, and could pick up the heartbeats of babies, record them, and note patterns. This was an interesting step forward, and we began to detect abnormal patterns. Doctor Hon at Yale Medical School began to note similar findings, and it soon became obvious that we also needed a way to record uterine contractions in relation to the heart-rate patterns. I began talking about the finding at various meetings, as did Caldeyro-Barcia and Hon.

Monitoring machines soon replaced mine, which was a first, so far as I could find. The monitoring machines recorded the uterine contractions, and at the same time the heart rates. We now began to be able to detect problems with the baby during labor. We also learned that if we took small samples of blood from the baby's scalp, we could measure the oxygen content of the blood, which was vital information. To get more accurate heart rates, an electrode was placed on the fetal scalp. Though we took advantage of all of this new knowledge, our early interest made my group quite authoritative on the subject of monitoring.

With our new knowledge of erythroblastosis and fetal monitoring, we were delivering more premature babies, and I decided that we had to improve our care of these little people, because so many were impaired or did not survive. We had a great opportunity. The chief of Pediatrics was at the end of his term, and we decided to put in charge of the nursery and the department a doctor interested in intensive care of the newborn. Our choice was Marguerite Markarian.

Immediately, there was a marked change. Doctor Markarian was an expert at treating the respiratory distress problems that premature infants developed. She also improved the prevention of the eye disease retrolental fibroplasia, which was often the cause of blindness or partial blindness of prematures. It seemed to have been related to the high levels of oxygen in the atmosphere provided to prematures. We began to save extremely small babies, and they did better and better. I went to the professor and chair of Obstetrics and Gynecology at UCSF to tell him about our intensive care nursery. Doctor Page said, "I see you are saving more babies, but what are you saving?" He implied, of course, that the babies we were saving would have great trouble, and would not be healthy children. In another year, we showed that our graduates from the intensive care nursery were doing as well or even better than those who were in the regular nursery. Doctor Page was finally convinced, and started an intensive care program of his own. Now, the University of California care of high-risk babies and the associated nursery was on a level with the best in the country.

Doctor Markarian was hired away from Mount Zion by a Texas school with a lot of money, and she continued to do outstanding work, but Mount Zion was able to replace her with Roberta Ballard, who improved the intensive care nursery, but at the same time supported vigorously the program that I was developing in prepared childbirth, which had minimal interference by obstetricians. She and I were interested in giving birth back to the mothers. She developed a successful program in which babies or pregnant women who faced early delivery were transported from far away. One of our residents, often with other support, would go to escort the patient or baby by plane or other transport to our hospital. This program was also financially a winner, and therefore was one of the first areas UCSF wanted after the merger of UC and Mount Zion. Doctor Ballard did not want to be part of the UC system, and moved elsewhere to continue her success.

While this was going on, I developed a staff of doctors who were skilled with high-risk pregnancies. They helped to improve our statistics and our teaching program. Sandy Levine was the best.

At this time one of our aims was to minimize prematurity by delaying the onset of labor. I had noted that ethyl alcohol as available in vodka, Scotch, bourbon, etc., relieved the discomfort of painful menstruation. It also seemed that relief was provided by the quieting of uterine contractions. I had a patient, a doctor's wife, who had lost a number of pregnancies so prematurely that the fetus never survived. I decided that I would try intravenous alcohol if she went into premature labor. I asked her to stay off her feet as much as possible, but in spite of that, she began to have contractions at a time when the baby would not be viable even with an intensive care nursery. I started a dilute alcohol drip intravenously, and contractions were minimal. I kept her in the hospital with minimal activity, with the alcohol drip going day and night. One day, as I approached her room, I heard her singing. She was "high" on the alcohol, but able to remain pregnant until the baby was viable. The baby was small but healthy; I recall that he had small feet, but he developed in a normal way. The patient and her husband were thrilled, and after a while were expecting a second child. We followed the same procedure; this time she got wildly drunk, but again the baby survived, and she now had a son and daughter. I persuaded her not to force her luck further. The perinatologists developed other medication to quiet premature contractions. They felt that the problems with alcohol were to be avoided, but we had delivered two healthy children.

I have a letter from the mother that I will quote in part:

"It seems appropriate that on this special day as Maya (the younger child) is one that our very special thoughts are of you. There isn't any adequate way to say 'Thank you' for our son-shine and our angel-shine. In the end we got exactly what we wanted. The journey to that end, however, was long and involved—so much work on the part of so many, but especially you; because at the end it was your decision which gave us Ravi-Evan and Maya.

"In some special way these are your children, too. Every smile they give out is a reflection of the rainbow of life you gave them. So on this special day we give you our love."

This was accompanied by a lovely picture of the two children together.

It is situations like this that make the practice of obstetrics especially enjoyable. There were so many other rewarding experiences.

In a way, it reminded me how I felt when I was a combat medic. During the war, I often said that if I saved one life, I had justified my being there. There turned out to be more such instances than I can remember, and they helped balance the horror I had when there was nothing I could do.

Chapter 8

Annie, 1980

My close friend Les Fink was a fine psychoanalyst. He volunteered at the Jewish Home for the Aged, where he provided much needed consultations for the staff and the inhabitants. One day he called me and asked if I would see a patient for whom he could find no medical care in the city of San Francisco. He told me that she was about seventy and had profound mental problems, but equally important, she had a massive vaginal prolapse. Of course, I agreed to see the patient, though I did not realize what a problem I was to face.

On the day of her first visit, Annie appeared. She was carrying a large sack of old clothes. She was thoroughly disheveled. Her hair was in disarray. Most of her teeth were missing, and her simple dress fitted poorly. She did not talk in a rational fashion. She did mention problems with her mother, and that she had had a child that died during childbirth. It took all my patience to get her to go to an examining room, where she refused to undress completely, but finally my nurse—after covering her with a sheet—was able to get Annie's underclothes off. Under the sheet, I found the largest prolapse I had ever seen. A prolapse is caused by damage to the supports of the pelvic organs. It is almost always caused by problems with obstetrical delivery injuring the supports of the pelvic organs. With this damage, the uterus and ovaries descend into the vagina, and the vagina essentially turns inside out. As the vaginal tissues get stretched, more and more of the abdominal content can enter the sac that is formed. It is rare to see anything as profound as this case. The sac protruding from the vagina extended to her knees. It contained her pelvic organs and a mass of bowel. Usually, efforts to control the prolapse are instituted, even in more primitive societies. Support inserts called pessaries have been used, and even filling the vagina with various materials was tried. In modern surgery, for over a hundred years there have been available various surgical procedures that are particularly effective, if carried out early. In this case, the mass coming from the vagina was eroded and foul-smelling. At the lower end was an atrophic cervix. Trying not to alarm her, I cleaned up the surface of the prolapse, and, carefully taking considerable time, I was able to reduce the mass—that is, get the bowel and vagina where they belonged. I then placed the largest pessary I had in the office. It was a large ring that folded and was inserted behind the pubic bone. We helped her up. She got dressed and came into my office. She noted the difference and seemed happy. Her escort from the home took her back there. The next day, I was called to say that the pessary had come out and so the prolapse recurred. I had Annie return at my first available chance. I was never sure whether the pessary had come out or whether the patient had pulled it out.

After trying the large ring pessary again with the same results, I decided that the only pessary that might work was a plastic cube. It has indentations on each side that provided suction. This pessary worked. However, when the patient came to have the pessary cleaned, there was a release of a huge amount of foul discharge when the cube was removed with considerable difficulty. After cleaning up the mess, I was not able to use the room again that day, because of the odor. So I reduced the prolapse again and placed a quantity of antibiotic cream in the vaginal space, and then replaced the cube. When it came time to replace the cube, in spite of the antibiotic cream, there was another outpouring of foul material. I could not use my examining room again that day. Removing the cube to clean it continued to be difficult. Finally, after some months, the patient refused further dealing with her problem in this way. Les pleaded with me to operate.

I had seen only one patient with a similar problem. My professor Herbert Traut was the physician in charge. He was one of the best gynecological surgeons in the country. He performed a vaginal hysterectomy and a repair. During the patient's convalescence, the suture line gave way, and the patient's intestines poured through the defect. In spite of all efforts, that patient died. Obviously, having seen this, I was reluctant to attempt a repair, especially with a patient who was psychotic and unlikely to be cooperative.

Les would not relent. He thought I should operate. I came up with a plan. First, we would devote weeks in trying to improve the surface of the prolapse to avoid infection. I insisted that caretakers known to the patient would be with her day and night. Finally, in planning the operation, I decided to leave the uterus so that there would not be a defect in the vault of the vagina through which the bowel could prolapse. I planned to examine the inside of the uterus during the operation to be sure there was no evidence of cancer. Then I would remove most of the epithelium that covered the prolapse, and construct a narrow vagina not much larger in diameter than a pencil. I did plan to remove the mouth of the uterus (the cervix) and to do a type of repair called a Manchester to improve support. This combination would allow for drainage with support, and I thought it would be less likely to allow the prolapse to recur. Of course, prophylactic antibiotics were to be used.

The operation took over four hours, which was a long operation for me. However, it went as planned. The next day the patient pleaded with me to remove the catheter that was in her bladder. I did not want to do that, because I feared that if the catheter was removed, the patient would not be able to urinate due to swelling in the area. She complained about the catheter repeatedly, and in spite of constant observation, she was able to pull the catheter out on the second postoperative day. The catheter was a Foley, a kind that had a little balloon on its end. I feared that pulling the catheter out might have ruined the repair, but fortunately the patient was able to urinate normally. She did well, in large part due to the emotional support she got from workers from the home.

Six weeks later she appeared in my office with her hair in place. She wore a clean neat dress and did not smell. She immediately gave me a big kiss. The repair held. I am told that, before the operation, other people at the home had stayed away from her; they now accepted her and her strange ways. That was one of the most satisfying experiences I had as a physician.

Chapter 9

Abortion, 1950

When I started private practice, I became aware of the terrible problems being generated by our national policy on abortion. I agreed to be a consultant at the San Francisco Hospital (the San Francisco General) UC Obstetrics and Gynecology Service. I found immediately that one of the main reasons for admission to that service was complications from criminal abortion.

Abortions at that time were illegal, though a few were permitted to save a mother's life. Almost all abortions were performed illegally, and the penalties for doing one were great. That being so, most abortions were performed by non-medical people. Those abortions were often complicated by hemorrhage from incomplete abortion, infection, perforation of the uterus, and severe damage to the vagina from caustic douches (by which it was hoped abortion could be induced). The staff on our service often had to complete incomplete abortions, with the hope of preventing hemorrhage or infection. The infections were particularly difficult to deal with. That was because we were limited in our use of antibiotics, which were in short supply. At the time penicillin, streptomycin, and tetracycline were available. There were many bacteria that did not respond to those three, particularly the anaerobes (those that can grow in a low-oxygen atmosphere). So, patients often developed abscesses and tubal infections in addition to infections in the uterus. We tried to avoid surgery, but it proved to be necessary when we could not control the infection with antibiotics and bed rest. Often we tried drainage, which also had its technical problems.

In the midst of this set of circumstances, I became aware that a close relative was very ill following a criminal abortion. She was young and unmarried. I was confronted with the problem of getting her care without her parents becoming aware. I had her admitted to The UC

Hospital under an assumed name. She was very ill with a high fever. She was treated vigorously with antibiotics, supervised by the superb infectious disease people at UCSF. She gradually recovered. However, when she was married later on, she was not able to get pregnant.

With this set of circumstances prevailing, I was faced with one of the worst problems in my life. I had a friend who lived north of San Francisco. He was married to a woman I had known well before the war. They had three children. She called me one day to say that she was pregnant. But then she told me that she had not slept with her husband for a number of months. To continue the pregnancy would result in the end of her marriage. I said that I was not familiar with her area. Did she know anyone she could trust to do an abortion? She said that she lived in a small community, and it would be dangerous to ask. She had asked her closest friend, who was of no help. I had her send a urine specimen down to confirm the diagnosis. We were doing a pregnancy test using rabbits at the time. The test was clearly positive. I finally agreed to do the procedure. She was in the habit of coming to San Francisco for dental care. That provided the excuse. I was able to get the proper equipment and drugs. With local anesthesia, I was able to do the procedure with ease in the evening in my office. The ease was related to the fact that she had had multiple pregnancies, which made it simple to dilate the cervix enough to do the procedure safely. This was a terrible emotional strain for me, and I developed the first of a series of neck spasms. She was fine and her marriage continued for a number of years before eventual divorce.

This whole series of events led me to become much more active in trying to make abortion more available. The practice of getting psychiatric consultations, with the thought that the danger of suicide would be a "threat to life," worked for a while. To expedite that sort of subterfuge, therapeutic abortion committees were instituted. Eventually, the psychiatrists began to revolt, since they could not demonstrate the association. None of them had seen a pregnant woman commit suicide.

Much to our delight, the Supreme Court of the United States agreed to the proposal of Roe vs. Wade. A woman's right to choose was established as the law of the land, though conservatives fought against that law.

Now, with abortion legal, we found that our practicing doctors had little experience doing the procedure, and even with hospital support, there were often serious problems. I heard that in Israel and Czechoslovakia there had been some successful use of suction to cause abortion. There was no literature, but I thought the procedure would be logical. I got the instrument maker at UC to make me a set of cannulas that could be introduced into the uterus so that the pregnancy could be evacuated with suction, and I tried the suction in the operating rooms. It didn't work. Then I had the engineers at Mount Zion make a suction machine that was more powerful. It worked. There were problems with the equipment from ease-of-use point of view. I began to lecture about the use of this technique. An organization in Berkeley decided to make equipment for the procedure. They developed plastic disposable cannulas and a better suction machine. We were now in the clear. The procedure of therapeutic abortion could be done in most cases in a much safer manner.

Unfortunately, there are those in the United States who would like to return to the old days by making abortion illegal. I abhor the possibility of seeing the kinds of problems we saw return.

Chapter 10

Childbirth

Throughout history, ways have been sought to make childbirth more comfortable for women. Early on, various narcotics were tried. Then there was the development of "twilight sleep," which involved the use of narcotics, along with scopolamine; this caused women to lose contact with reality, and often become violent. In Boston, women in labor were often put in a hammock placed in the bed to avoid injuring themselves. The babies born to these women were often depressed, and slow to breathe and cry. There then was a move toward significant doses of sleep medications with some narcotic. This was supplemented with intermittent use of nitrous oxide and anesthetic gas administered with relatively low levels of oxygen. This was usually supplemented by various forms of local anesthesia in the vaginal area.

Just prior to our involvement in World War II, attempts were made in the use of anesthesia to block the nerves to the lower abdomen without interfering with uterine function. Two routes were tried. An associate and I tried paravertebral block, which blocked the nerves as they entered the spinal cord. We had difficulty in getting prolonged effect, though the anesthesia worked. At the same time, another approach was developed, caudal anesthesia. This involved introducing anesthetic agents into the caudal space near the tailbone. A flexible needle permitted easy refill as needed, and the space held a good quantity of anesthetic agent. This was improved by using a catheter inserted through the needles. Women were now able to go through labor with little or no discomfort. This technique was improved by the development of epidural block, which is similar to the caudal, but applied higher in the back. This provided even more elegant control of pain, because there could be a more accurate administration of the anesthetic agent. But there were problems. Occasionally, the anesthetic would interfere with respiration. Also, if given early, the block often stopped labor. Sometimes labor was prolonged. Most of the time forceps were used for delivery, because the mother, having little or no sensation, was deprived of the urge to bear down, which is necessary for spontaneous delivery.

There developed a movement among some women for the return to natural childbirth. In England, Grantly Dick Read promoted the idea of prepared childbirth, in which women approached birthing in a more natural way, after having had careful education in techniques that would help tolerance. In England and on the continent, many babies were born at home. Though that deprived the mother of the safety factors provided by the hospital, it did provide a more relaxed environment than that provided by hospitals.

I found that increasing numbers of parents and prospective parents had been concerned that medical care of women in labor had interfered with the natural process of childbirth, and had been replaced with too much physician interference in delivery of the baby. Those concerns, plus rising costs, renewed interest in home births.

In 1973, I decided that we should provide prepared childbirth as an alternative for low-risk mothers. An alternative birth center had been tried at the San Francisco County Hospital, but it had had minimal community support. Although I greatly sympathized with the patients who wished to give birth in as simple and satisfying way as possible, and to keep costs down, I did not believe it advisable to risk delivery away from the support and safety features that had been developed in the last hundred or more years. I decided the alternative birth center would provide a response to a real need.

As I was developing this point of view, I began to use some of the ideas in our regular setting. The first was to allow fathers in the delivery room. This had been proposed by two of my friends, Doctors Volmer and Marsh, who were qualified in obstetrics, gynecology and psychiatry. Our decision to do this was met with a storm of protest from many of the physicians in the community. At that time, fathers often could not be with their wives while they were in labor. Most doctors felt that the father's presence would be dangerous. He might cause a disturbance; he might contaminate the area. I found that the fathers were very supportive of their wives or partners; they did not cause trouble, and there was no increase in infection. Under certain trying circumstances, the fathers were asked to leave the delivery room. I also began to dispense with stirrups, which had become standard equipment for most deliveries in the United States. (This did not mean that there was no place for stirrups.)

Now I was ready. The first requirement was to provide a room that would serve as both a labor and delivery room, in which the patient could have the support of the father and others, including professionals. Midwives were vital at this point, and ours was the first private hospital in San Francisco to have midwives working in their profession in the hospital. A homelike atmosphere was essential, but necessary equipment for care of the mother and child had to be accommodated in an inconspicuous area of the room.

Adequate safety factors were a prime consideration. These began with location of the room within a few yards of the regular labor and delivery area, where there were modern monitors in every room. Full-time, in-house anesthesia coverage was available for emergency. A superior nursery was close by. We had the support of our house staffs in obstetrics and pediatrics. Probably the most important factor was one-to-one nursing by nurses trained and skilled in techniques of prepared childbirth. These nurses also followed the patients after discharge.

To create a comfortable, homelike atmosphere, the alternative birth room was furnished with chairs, tables, plants, music, and instrument cabinets of a quality seen in homes rather than hospitals. The room also had a sofa bed for any support person who might need it. We had a good light source and an incubator. We used a regular double bed with a firm mattress for delivery and labor, and the mother was permitted to walk around if she desired. Or, if she preferred sitting in a chair or even squatting, that was fine with us. We had a simple set of instruments for the delivery, and occasionally we moved the mother to the end of the bed for ease of delivery.

If any problem developed, the mother was transferred to the regular labor and delivery area.

The program was a huge success, and we almost doubled the number of deliveries expected. We soon had to build a second room. We developed a dedicated staff.

One of the great sights of my life was on the morning after the birth of my second grandchild. His older sister had been the first born in our birthing room. As I walked in the door. There in bed together were the new baby boy, his mother, his father, and his sister. I was so pleased.

These techniques are now followed widely in the United States and Canada. We had given the joy of delivering a baby back to the mother.

Chapter 11

Travel

After the war, I encouraged my parents to travel to Europe. I made reservations for them and suggested an itinerary for their first trip. I suggested Claridge's in London, the Ritz in Paris, The Gritti in Venice, The Grand in Florence, and The Hassler in Rome. They loved them all. My mother bought quite a lot, and after giving her children generous gifts of sweaters, furniture, and souvenirs, found that she could sell the remaining furniture and decorative pieces quickly, since she was an interior decorator. That prompted her and my dad to go to Europe almost every year, and to begin trips to the Orient. All of that stimulated our interest. I, of course, was anxious to show Gwen around the areas I had been in during World War II.

Our first of eighty-three trips was in September 1958. It was difficult for us to leave our children, but Gwen's widowed mother agreed to stay at our house, along with Mary, who worked for us on a daily basis.

Those were the days of prop planes. We flew to New York, where we were taken off the plane to the Golden Door restaurant for breakfast. We then flew to London in nine hours and ten minutes. Gwen loved everything about England, though she and I found London run-down. They still had not filled many of the gaps caused by The Blitz. On the other hand, there were flowers in flower boxes everywhere, and some areas were quite elegant, like the Burlington Arcade and Bond Street. It is difficult to think of those times without remembering the curiosity we had. We wanted to see everything. An example: One day we went by train to Windsor Castle. We did a complete tour there. We got a bus to The Mitre Inn, which is across from Hampton Court, where we went after lunch. We followed the route we had suggested for my parents, but we stayed in much less expensive hotels. It is interesting to note that dinner at Mirabelle for two was $11.60. The average cab fare was forty cents. On the way to Paris, I was quite ill with a fever, but I did not tell Gwen. I did not have time to be ill. Near us in Paris was a small restaurant, La Troute. It specialized in "chicken on a string" (a chicken grilled while hanging on a string, which caused it to rotate). They had a wonderful chicken soup, which I ordered to start my first meal in France. My fever broke, and I was well from then on. Who says there is no magic in chicken soup? In Paris, I could hardly wait to take Gwen to St. Chapelle, which I had "found" on my first trip to Paris during the war. At this time, traffic in Paris was relatively light, and I drove a Citroën 2CV, the top of which went up and down like a window shade. The car was much smaller than any I had ever driven, so on one occasion I missed seeing a stoplight. A gendarme stopped me, and I was sure he was going to send me to jail. However, he at last let me go without even a fine. After that I was more careful. Of course, we visited all of the major sites with three stars in the Michelin. We even had a three-star dinner at Lapérouse. Our plan was to have one three-star, one two-star, and one one-star meal. They were all superb, and I will always remember the Grand Marnier soufflé at Lapérouse. It is difficult to believe that we traveled to Versailles and Fontainebleau, with stops at well-known restaurants like that at Montfort-l'Amaury. But somehow, Italy was special!

Our plane was late getting from Paris to Milan, so the airline decided to take all the passengers to lunch. (Can you imagine that now?) It was a lovely warm day, and we were taken to a restaurant where we ate under a grape arbor. We were first served large dishes of pasta with sturdy red wine, and we thought that that was a fine lunch. To our surprise, that was followed with a full luncheon. We took the train to Venice, where we arrived after dark. At the train station we got a gondola to take us to our hotel, The Regina et di Roma. It was a beautiful, quiet night with a full moon. We did not want the ride to end. (In those days, gondolas were inexpensive.) The hotel had been recommended by friends, and we asked for a specific room, which we got. The room was nice, but not remarkable, until I opened the French doors. There was a huge deck looking directly across the canal to Santa Maria della Salute. It was a sight we would never forget. Our friends Phyllis and Maury Barusch had a similar room (there were two such) and they joined us for champagne. I had won a bottle on our flight for guessing the length of the flight from the United States. In Venice I switched from black-and-white film to color, and I guess that is the way travelers feel when they get to Italy. There is no need to go on about the charms of Venice. At that time, there was no scaffolding, and no crowds of tourists. Reluctantly, we left and went by train to Florence. The most unusual thing we did was to go to a special event for the foreign ministers of the various Mediterranean countries. Gwen and I were dressed in our best, having gone to one of the more elegant restaurants. As we were walking from dinner in the main square, we noted that the palace was lighted.

We had been there earlier in the day, at which time we had seen workers busily preparing for something important. We approached the entrance, where on the main staircase stands a lion of Florence with a wreath of flowers on his head. There were flower garlands on the main staircase. Gwen was reluctant to go in, but I thought we could do no harm, and since we were so well-dressed, we could easily be guests. No one stopped us as we climbed the stairs. The palace, which is usually quite austere, was alight with indirect lighting and candles. There were buffets at various points. (Gwen would not let me touch anything.) There was music. We wandered around, looked at the elegant people, and noted how much more beautiful the palace was under these circumstances. Reluctantly, we left and returned to our hotel, which faced the Arno. We had a huge room on the top floor. While in Florence we found time to travel to Pisa with a friend of my parents, Georgio. We had another charming experience. A man with whom my mother had worked offered to drive us to the seashore. On the way, he picked up an attractive woman, and when Gwen and I assumed that she must be his wife, we were told amidst much laughter that she was his "lady." We had a superb seafood meal at the shore. I could not believe the amount his lady was able to consume. Reluctantly, we left Florence for Rome, where we stayed in the small Pensione Pfister. It was at the top of the Spanish Steps, across from the Hotel Hassler Roma. We had a room with a sink, a toilet, and a douche bowl, but the shower and tub were down the hall. Though they were shared, we did not have a problem. Outside our room was a deck that looked over the city, and there we had breakfast, which was included in our cost of approximately four dollars a day. Before breakfast, I crossed the street to the Hassler, where the concierge knew my parents. He made reservations for me, and gave me The Herald

Tribune daily—all of which was luxurious. I had rented the smallest Fiat, and we were able to drive around Rome. That was a wild experience, but somehow we managed. In retrospect, it is hard for me to believe that we did as much as we did. We saw the major sites of Rome, and had a chance to go to the funeral of Pius XII. It is difficult to choose the most impressive; however, St. Peter's, the Vatican, St.Paul's Outside the Walls, the Piazza Navona, and the Trevi Fountain come quickly to mind.

It was time to return home. We learned a good deal from that first trip. We got to know each other in a different way, and we found that we enjoyed the discovery that came with travel. We planned more trips, and we thought that our future travels should be a little less ambitious. There were over eighty more. It would not be proper at this point to talk about each of the trips, but certainly there are a few that were particularly memorable and I will mention them briefly.

In 1974, we went to Egypt, after a stop in Rome. The trip was with an English company, Swan. We arrived in Cairo a couple of days early, and we resolved to be careful of what we ate or drank. I had already begun to write for the local paper, the Chronicle, and health tips for travelers. I suggested that only bottled water, bottled drinks, or boiled water—as with hot tea or hot coffee—were to be drunk. I also advised that food that should be hot must be hot, and if it was not, it should be sent back. It was wise not to drink or eat dairy products at that time, and certainly mayonnaise should be avoided. The Hilton Hotel was next door to the Cairo Museum. The museum had a great collection, but we were advised to take flashlights. We joined the group on a small river boat reminiscent of the boat in "Death on the Nile." There was no air conditioning. The doors to the cabins were screens, to which we attached an electric fan, but the days were warm. I soon found that we were to be traveling with a remarkable group. Our leader, Sir Cyril Aldred, had written a number of books on Egypt, and he could read hieroglyphs like I read the newspaper. He divided our group into "The Scouts," who were archeologists traveling with us, "The Light Infantry," which included Gwen and me, and "The Tourists." Our group was to go everywhere, no matter how hot it was, nor how difficult the terrain. Sir Cyril was to lead us. A wonderful Egyptian guide was to lead the last group. We would leave early in the morning to avoid the heat. We returned for late lunch, and spent the afternoon on the top deck under an awning, watching the Egyptians onshore acting much like they did 2,000 years before.

Because of the heat, we ran out of bottled water. Until then, Gwen and I had limited ourselves to bottled water, beer, or tea. Our group was assured that the boat had modern water-purifying equipment. It looked impressive, but in retrospect, I do not think the Egyptian crew knew how to clean it. Our passengers began to get sick. The doctor on board ran out of anti-diarrhea medication. Unfortunately, some of our passengers were unable to make it to some of the best sites. So, I decided to share my store of medication with my fellow passengers. Fortunately, I had enough, and I found an extremely grateful group. Gwen and I remained well.

We stopped at those remarkable sites that all travelers who go to Egypt marvel at. Certainly the tombs were most memorable for me. The splendid Tut artifacts in the Cairo Museum had just returned from a world tour. We found it so sad that they were displayed so poorly.

It was one of the most stimulating groups I had ever been with. There was an archeologist who had been in the Middle East for years, a professor of history from The University of Oklahoma, a wonderful Mormon couple who had spent time working in Israel, and a couple who became friendly with us who we later found out were first cousins to The Queen. The talk on deck covered a wide range, and I learned from all the passengers. It was a small group, around twenty-five, so we got to know each other, and the cocktail hour enhanced our mutual knowledge. When I could, I studied for the Gynecologic Oncology Boards, which I planned to take on my way home with a stop in Chicago.

On the way to Chicago, I got sick in spite of all my care. I could control my symptoms, but I knew I had picked up something. Gwen remained well. When I reported to take the boards, I felt terrible, but I was able to pass everything except a portion that had to do with irradiation therapy. I did not know enough about dose calculation, which I had been in the habit of leaving up to the radiologists. I was offered a chance to take that portion of the examination separately. This was the first time these boards were given, and fortunately for me, I was treated with respect. I think the examiners also recognized that I was not well when I was taking the oral portion. When I got home, first examinations of me seemed to indicate that I had amoebic infection plus Giardia. More careful study revealed that the amoeba was a benign form, but therapy had already begun with large doses of Flagyl. The dose was cut, but sadly to say, I was still on the drug as the holidays began, and I was unable to take any alcohol. I often wonder how my safety precautions broke down, and I believe when I was told that the water purifier was the best, I probably had some ice in a drink. I learned to distrust the knowledge of the crew in caring for the apparatus too late. Gwen was smarter, but she too, had Giardia. When I was in medical school, we were taught that Giardia was a benign parasite. I am here to say that it is not.

In spite of the problems that arise on every trip, I find that I have enjoyed "seeing the world," and while doing that, forgetting the trials and tribulations associated with medical practice.

Chapter 12

Sam

When I was a senior at Cal, my father gave me his membership at Lake Merced Golf Club. All of his old golfing partners had died, and he now was making new friends who had a common interest in all kinds of fishing. I was a fair-to-good golfer, but I did not have much time to play. However, one of the people I got to play with was a young lawyer named Sam Ladar. At first I did not know much about him except what I knew about his impressive golfing ability (much better than mine), his obvious knowledge, and his camaraderie. When I returned from the war, we took up golfing together some; however, I had to devote most of my time to residency training. Finally, when I went into practice, I needed a lawyer. I knew two other lawyers, Ben Lehrer and John Golden, both of whom took on high-profile cases, but I decided that Sam was the man I needed, and it was an excellent choice.

By that time, Sam had begun to have an established position in our community. He worked with great energy doing a variety of services pro bono. I learned more and more about him. He went to UC Berkeley and later to Boalt Hall, the prestigious law school at UC. He had been an outstanding athlete at Cal, and he was the model for a book about those times.

After I had been in practice awhile, I had a partner, and moved close to Mount Zion Hospital, where I did most of my work. This made it possible for me to play a bit more golf. My friend Alan Abrams convinced me that I should take golf lessons from a pro at the California Golf Club, Art Bell. My handicap rapidly dropped to a respectable 12. Now, I was free to play with Sam and other good players like my friend Les Fink without feeling completely outclassed. Golfing together, Sam and I developed an even closer friendship. When a new clubhouse was built, we asked that our lockers be next to each other.

Pauline (my secretary since I started practice) was pregnant, so I hired a young woman who was efficient and well-liked by my patients. After a year or so, she was engaged to marry a young man from a good family in the Midwest. My wife and I bought her a silver tray from Gump's for a wedding gift. When I hired a new person to take her place, the new woman, Kathy, found in checking the books that the woman before her had obviously been stealing cash that was paid into the office. She figured that the amount was about $15,000, which was a lot in those days. I called Sam. He said that I should meet him at once at the District Attorney's office. I said that I had patients to see. He said that I should arrange for them to be seen, but that he would meet me as soon as possible in the DA's office.

The district attorney found out almost at once that my former employee had left the state and had moved to Michigan with her new husband. He said that it was impossible for us to extradite her from there to California; however, if she ever came to California to let him know. I found the address of my former employee and wrote to her, but I got no answer.

I had just about written off the money I was owed when one day one of my patients told me she had seen my former employee in Southern California, apparently visiting her mother for Thanksgiving. I called Sam, who contacted the district attorney. On the day before Thanksgiving, he had the woman arrested and put in jail. Her husband called me, indignant that I had taken such an action. He even said if he had known I was going to be so mean, he would have paid the money owed me. He suggested he pay me the money over a period of time. I said the whole matter was out of my hands, and that he would have to deal with the district attorney in San Francisco. The next day, even though it was a holiday, the DA called me to ask if I would be happy just to get the money with no further action by him, Mr. Ladar, or me. I said that would be fine. A couple of days later I got a cashier's check for the exact amount that had been stolen. I give full credit in that matter to Sam, who was respected by the district attorney, who in turn acted efficiently, probably not for me so much as for Sam.

Over the years, when I had major decisions to make, I usually consulted my parents. I felt that my father was very practical, and knew about the business world. After my Dad died in 1971, Sam became my major consultant on matters non-medical. He was the most ethical person I have ever known, and his guidance was invaluable. I think the only bill I ever got from him was when he wrote a partnership agreement for me. That agreement proved to be most valuable.

Sam's wife, Sylvia, became a patient of mine. She had been a patient of Alice Maxwell, who was one of the very best, and I was honored in having recovered well. She was a perfect partner for Sam. They had been close since their years in college.

Sam and I began to play golf together regularly on Saturdays. We had a wonderful foursome with Jack Davis and Stan Breyer. Out lockers were close together. We played our hearts out in competition for a few dollars, but we had great times.

Sam developed cancer of the pancreas, for which there was no treatment. But he kept going as long as he could, and I recall a pleasant dinner we had with him and Sylvia at Perry's only a few nights before he died. He never complained.

Among others, I spoke at his funeral and said the following:

"It was the big basketball game between California and Stanford. It was the last game of the season. The championship was also at stake. The great athlete Ernie Nevers was playing for Stanford, and Sam Ladar was the star of the Golden Bears. There were only a few seconds left in the game, which was tied. Sam had a free shot. If he sank that shot, Cal would win, and the game would be over. The pavilion was wild. Sam pumped up. He let the ball fly in an unusually high arc toward the basket. It hit the rim and bounced over the backboard. You can imagine how Sam and the Cal rooters felt at that point. The game went into overtime. Stanford got the tipoff. However, according to Ben Lom, Sam stole the ball. He dribbled down the court, spun, set, and shot. This time the ball went through the basket without touching the rim. The game was over; Cal had won. The stands went wild. Sam got off the court as fast as he could through the congratulating crowd. All he really wanted to do then was to be with Sylvia and to get away.

"About a year ago, Sam and I were playing golf as a team. He was beginning to lose strength. We were on the last hole. Our match was tied. We were playing for our usual large sums (four or five dollars were at stake). The green was protected by a large trap. To win, Sam would have to clear the trap, but not be too far from the hole. He selected his club and carefully wiped the blade. He took a couple of practice swings. He then made a perfect shot, which ended close enough to make the putt and win the match for our team. One of our opponents knocked the ball away and said, "That's good, Sam." Sam said, "You shouldn't have done that. You take away the fun. You take away meeting the challenge." He put the ball down and made the putt.

These events, though almost a lifetime apart, tell you a great deal about Sam. He faced the challenges of life with intensity, whether they involved sports, his profession, or volunteer work, and even committees (for which he was always well-prepared). He faced death that way too.

He didn't expect anyone to give him anything, even a putt, and certainly not kudos. He probably would have been embarrassed by all this today.

He was an inspiration and a father figure for me, and I am sure for many others. He and Sylvia made the greatest team I've ever known.

If I may borrow from our liturgy: As long as I live, when I am on a golf course, when I hear a lucid argument, when I see a graceful athlete, most important when I must make an ethical decision I, like many of you, will think of Sam."

Chapter 13

1975

In 1975, I was elected Chief of Staff at the Mount Zion Medical Center. Almost immediately, I was faced with the problem of the rising costs of malpractice insurance. I wrote the following to the San Francisco Chronicle, which published it:

"A SOLUTION NEEDED

"Editor: I am appalled by the apparent lack of interest shown by the news media in the problems of malpractice insurance for doctors. The average physician doing a surgical specialty is faced with a tremendous rise in premiums. In my office of three physicians, the premiums will rise from approximately $13,000 per year to approximately $55,000 a year. This outrageously high charge will cause a number of problems. Many physicians will be unable to meet the premiums, since they will not be able to raise fees enough to cover the costs. The patients who pay doctors will be faced with markedly increased fees, which their insurance carriers are unlikely to fund at this time.

"Faced with the problem, many physicians are choosing to leave practice until some equitable solution has been worked out. This may well result in the closure of some hospital facilities for all but acute care. Certainly, the public will suffer.

"There must be a public demand for legislative correction of this situation.

"JOHN A. KERNER, M.D.

"San Francisco"

On April 30, 250 anesthesiologists in fifty bay area counties went on strike and would only give anesthesia for emergencies, not including normal childbirth. Many other doctors joined them by not hospitalizing patients except in emergencies. Some even closed their offices except for emergencies. This was a disaster for the hospitals. Their margin of profit usually came from elective surgery. They all began at once to bleed dollars. The medical societies appealed for help from the state, but nothing seemed to happen. There were no laws in California concerning malpractice insurance. The situation was covered as a major national story.

The Los Angeles Times reported as follows:

"A physicians' strike over skyrocketing malpractice insurance rates shut down operating rooms for all but emergency surgery Thursday at 50 Bay Area hospitals. Leading the 'stay home' protest were 250 anesthesiologists in five Bay Area counties. They refused to pay premiums that quadrupled for them as of midnight.

"They arranged, however, for at least one anesthesiologist to be on duty at each of the hospitals for emergency surgery." April 30 (1975)

Then came a surprising event.

My wife Gwen and I were playing golf on a Sunday. A man from the pro shop came on to the course to inform me that they had received a call that the governor, Jerry Brown, wanted to talk with me. I went to the pro shop and called the number that had been left. When I asked where and when, I was told to come to the State Building as soon as possible. I left the golf club at once, stopped by my office to pick up material I had been working on, and headed for the California State Building in the Civic Center. At the door, I was greeted by a police officer, who informed me the governor was waiting for me in the conference room, and I was escorted there.

Entering the room, which was impressive, being large and finely paneled, I expected to see other San Francisco physicians. I was the only doctor there. Sitting in front of the room was the governor, surrounded by a number of members of his staff at a long table: chief spokesman Gray Davis (later governor); Insurance Commissioner Wes Kinder; Director of Public Health Jerome Lackner; Deputy Secretary Robert Gnaizda; legal assistant Tony Klein; assistant legal assistant Alice Daniel; Secretary for Transportation and Business Don Burns; Lackner's assistant, Stuart Snyder; and Assemblyman Alister McAlister.

Governor Brown asked me what I thought he should do about the strike. It was important that something be done quickly, because important medical care was being denied, since it was not classified as "emergency." An example was presented in the San Francisco Chronicle and the Los Angeles Times. A woman suspected of having an abdominal cancer was denied surgery. That situation was not listed in the emergency list, and further delay could endanger her life. I said that the governor should make a strong public statement stating what he proposed to do, and that such a statement might induce the anesthesiologists to call off their strike. He asked what he should say in his statement. I suggested that there be a $250,000 limit on judgments for "pain and suffering," and that premiums be rolled back because of that. Also, there should be a shorter time limit for the filing of malpractice claims. After each of my suggestions, Brown spoke into a phone on his desk (which I later found was connected to someone from the trial lawyers group). He would say, "The doctor here says . . . " He did not tell me the responses.

After a while, the governor left the room, and members of his cabinet quizzed me for about an hour. I stressed the importance of something being done at the state level, since medical care was in turmoil. The hospitals were in increasing financial difficulty. The governor returned, stating he would consider the suggestions I had made.

The Chicago Daily News reported on April 30, "Doctor John Kerner, chief of staff at Mount Zion Hospital in San Francisco, said that he believes that doctors would go back to work if the governor makes a strong statement."

When I left, I called the president of the California Medical Association and the president of the San Francisco Medical Society to tell them what I had done.

A month went by, and there was no word from Sacramento. Problems increased. Because I was an obstetrician, I found it difficult to practice with no available anesthesiologist except for emergencies. Obstetrical emergencies are never expected. Though I could get anesthesiologists to be "on call," I could not get them to keep one of their group in the hospital. That got me in a position where I did a cesarean section with local anesthesia, and I gave caudal anesthesia

DIANNE FEINSTEIN
909 MONTGOMERY STREET, SUITE 400
SAN FRANCISCO, CA 94133

TELEPHONE: (415) 433-1333

June 9, 1992

John A. Kerner, M.D.
Second Floor
1545 Divisadero Street
San Francisco, CA 94115

Dear John,

Thank you so much for taking the time to write and
say congratulations.

I must say, winning is much better than losing.

Now, on to November. It's hard to believe that
one spends all of one's time, energy, and effort
just to get into the ring for the match but,
that's where we are now.

Your support, advice and help is more important
than ever.

Again, thank you for writing.

Warmest regards.

Cordially,

Dianne

Thanks John

Prof. Herbert Traut

Mike Bishop, Chancellor, University of California,
San Francisco, and me

Sam Ladar

Barbara Boxer and me

AT&T Ballpark, home of the San Francisco Giants,
the day honoring my son

Banquet honoring me in Normandy, France

Me and my brother Bob

Mary Jane Brinton

Judy Nadel, me, and Gwen

Daughter Jan, Granddaughter Lisa

Robert Wallerstein, Donald Magrin

Back to the site of
my aid station in
Bastogne

Me and John Chan,
Kerner Distinguished
Professor

BARBARA BOXER
CALIFORNIA

COMMITTEES:
APPROPRIATIONS
BANKING, HOUSING, AND
URBAN AFFAIRS
BUDGET
ENVIRONMENT
AND PUBLIC WORKS

United States Senate

HART SENATE OFFICE BUILDING
SUITE 112
WASHINGTON, DC 20510–0505
(202) 224–3553
senator@boxer.senate.gov
http://www.senate.gov/~boxer

May 29, 1998

Department of Obstetrics, Gynecology
and Reproductive Sciences
UCSF/Mount Zion Medical Center
2330 Post Street, Ste. 200
San Francisco, CA 94143-1688

Dear Friends:

It is a pleasure to have this opportunity to join you in
celebrating the remarkable life and career of Dr. John Kerner. I only
wish that I could be with you to thank him personally for all he has
meant to his city, his profession and his patients. His is deserving
of every honor and expression of admiration he receives tonight.

Dr. Kerner's association with UCSF/Mt. Zion Hospital and Medical
Center stretches back to his school days. He graduated UCSF medical
school in 1943, and after a period of decorated duty in the military,
he came home and completed his residency at UCSF in 1949. He became
board certified in Obstetrics and Gynecology in 1951.

The rest, as is often said, is history--the history of a gifted
scholar, teacher, administrator, and most important of all, doctor.
For no matter what else he was involved in, Dr. Kerner's first priority
has always been his patients, those people who trusted him enough to
place their very health and the health of their families in his hands.
As one of those patients, I consider myself truly blessed.

Dr. Kerner is a physician's physician. He is a warm, caring,
compassionate man who has devoted a half a century to bringing life,
health and healing to others. To look at him or listen to him, you'd
never suspect that Dr. Kerner is approaching his 80th birthday, he is
so young at heart. Perhaps it is precisely his generous spirit that
makes him so vibrant? If so, it is but one more example of how Dr.
Kerner's life and career can inform our own.

I hope you have a wonderful celebration.

Sincerely,

Barbara Boxer
United States Senator

☐ 1700 MONTGOMERY STREET
SUITE 240
SAN FRANCISCO, CA 94111
(415) 403-0100

☐ 2250 EAST IMPERIAL HIGHWAY
SUITE 545
EL SEGUNDO, CA 90245
(310) 414-5700

☐ 650 CAPITOL MALL
SUITE 6844
SACRAMENTO, CA 95814
(916) 448-2787

☐ 2300 TULARE STREET
SUITE 130
FRESNO, CA 93721
(209) 497-5109

☐ 525 B STREET
SUITE 990
SAN DIEGO, CA 92101
(619) 239-3884

☐ 210 NORTH E STREET
SUITE 210
SAN BERNARDINO, CA 92401
(909) 888-8525

**The Department of Obstetrics,
Gynecology & Reproductive Sciences**

Dr. A. Eugene Washington

**Saturday, April 17, 2004
The Westin St. Francis**

Museum of the Kansas National Guard

Home of the 35ᵗʰ Infantry Division Museum
P O Box 19285
Topeka, Kansas 66619-0285

(785) 862-1020   kngmuseum@aol.com

October 4, 2011

Dr. (Capt) John A. Kerner
1177 California St., #1410
San Francisco, CA 94108

Dear Dr. Kerner,

It was a pleasure talking with you on the telephone today, and we congratulate you and your family on your upcoming induction into the 35ᵗʰ Infantry Division Hall of Fame in September, 2012, at the Kansas City Airport Hilton Hotel, Kansas City, MO.

The 35ᵗʰ Division Hall of Fame is located in the 35ᵗʰ Division Museum at the Museum of the Kansas National Guard, 6700 SW Topeka Ave, Topeka, KS.

You will be in the fourth class to be inducted. Among the 28 previous inductees are three Medal of Honor recipients, President Harry S. Truman, Major General Paul Baade (who commanded the 35ᵗʰ Division throughout World War II), and many others.

As I indicated in our telephone conversation, I would greatly appreciate your assistance as we notify other of your family members and friends and invite them to the Induction Ceremony.

To assist us with the induction, we are in need of the following information, which may be submitted via e-mail or U. S. mail:

John Kerner is former Chief of Obstetrics, Gynecology and Reproductive Sciences at Mount Zion and a distinguished leader of the San Francisco medical community. He has contributed to the education of an entire generation of obstetrician/gynecologists and has fostered research and innovation in women's health. Together with his colleagues, family, and former patients, he has established both the John A. Kerner Endowed Chair and the John A. Kerner Distinguished Professorship in the UCSF Division of Gynecologic Oncology, focused on research in the area female reproductive tract cancers.

In June 1944, Dr. Kerner landed at Omaha Beach in Normandy shortly after D-Day, and spent the next 264 days in active combat in France, Belgium, Luxembourg and Normandy. He was awarded the Combat Medic Award, two Bronze Stars, five Battle Stars, and a Presidential Unit Citation. Most recently, his role in the Liberation of France was recognized by the President of France, Nicholas Sarkozy. On November 6, 2007, President Sarkozy bestowed the Legion d'Honneur upon Dr. Kerner in a special ceremony in Washington D.C.

The UCSF Department of Obstetrics, Gynecology & Reproductive Sciences Health congratulates Dr. Kerner on the extraordinary honor bestowed upon him by President Sarkozy and thanks him for his life long dedication to women's health.

advancing health worldwide™

University of California
San Francisco

National Center of Excellence
in Women's Health

Son John

Son Jim

Gerson and
Barbara Bass Bakar

French Legion of Honor

myself, which was risky from a malpractice point of view. Finally, one of the members of my department who had considerable experience with caudal anesthesia agreed to help. I made repeated calls to the Governor's office. Two groups of doctors decided to explore the possibility of forming their own malpractice companies.

At this point, I wrote the following to the San Francisco Chronicle:

"As the medical crisis continues, it is vital to define the true issues. The fundamental issue is not dollars. It is morality. In our country, the consumer wants and needs physicians to protect his medical interests. The consumer respects physicians and their integrity. No other profession has policed itself and improved itself as has medicine. No other profession is so respected. True, physicians have made errors, have at times been greedy, and are often naive politically. The individual responsibility and integrity of the physician has not been relinquished.

"The physician does not want, nor does his patient want, lawyers, insurance companies, or legislators to be the ones who protect patients interests. Therein lies the dilemma. Is it moral to withhold from patients the best care, to permit fine institutions and programs to face bankruptcy, to have large numbers of people out of work, while returning to practice under a system which has not protected the best interests of the patient? Or, is it moral to withhold services until the physicians are quite sure that their patients can be cared for in the highest tradition of medicine?

"The public must address itself to these issues NOW, or we never again will have medicine at the responsible level this country has come to know and to demand.

"Yours sincerely,
"John A. Kerner, M.D."

Fortunately, the situation was not entirely without humor. I got this letter from my friend Will Glickman.

"Dear John,
"Minding our own business last night, watching the TV news: There was a fellow on who claimed to be Dr. John Kerner of Mt. Zion

Hospital in San Francisco. Horty [his wife] started yelling, at that moment our phone rang so, I didn't get your words exactly straight. As I understand it, you have been traded to the Oakland A's for a left handed pitcher, correct? But, you looked great, See you soon. Will"

A month after my meeting at the State Building, I got word from someone in the Governor's office that he was proposing to the state legislature all of the suggestions I had made. The presentation was to be made by Alister McAlister. Obviously, they were not all my ideas, but I was the one chosen to present them. I said that the decision was great, but that it was too bad that action had not been taken sooner. The hospitals had lost large sums and I felt there had probably been damage to some patients because of insufficient care. Most important is the fact that the hospitals of San Francisco never recovered from the cash drain—all of which could have been prevented by more prompt action by Governor Brown. I have always felt that his decision was delayed by the trial lawyers.

The anesthesiologists agreed to go back to work for ninety days, after which they would reassess the situation. They joined those of us who had decided that forming our own insurance companies would be a good idea. If proper legislation was passed, with careful selection of doctors to be insured, we were sure that we could provide lower premiums. Of course, the key would be legislation. The program passed our legislature. California has set an example for the nation in dealing with medical malpractice. The trial lawyers are still unhappy in California. In other states, trial lawyers have been successful in resisting malpractice insurance reform.

Of interest is the following from the Wall Street Journal of Oct. 8:

"Limited Damage

"A study of a 1975 California law capping malpractice awards for noneconomic damages, such as pain and suffering at $250,000, found that:

"The law reduced the overall liability of defendants by 30 percent.

"The median reduction in awards for noneconomic damages is $366,000.

"Injured babies under one year old had reductions imposed in 71 percent of their cases.

"The median reduction for this group was $1.5 million.

"Plaintiffs 65 years of age and older had awards reduced 67 percent of the time."

Finally, after 29 years with national medical costs rising, the country is beginning to realize that we began to solve the problem in California in 1975.

* * *

We were faced with another problem. Our hospital and most others would not permit doctors on their staffs unless they had adequate malpractice insurance. A group of doctors protested. The hospitals responded that if they permitted doctors on their staffs without malpractice insurance, the hospital would have to carry enough extra insurance to cover those physicians. The cost would be devastating for the hospitals. Eventually, the striking doctors gave in. This was in part due to the development of doctor-owned insurance companies that lower the premiums even further than would have been possible with just the passage of the malpractice reform legislation.

* * *

It was an exciting time for me. On the other hand, in addition to my duties as chief of staff, I continued to work in my office, though on restricted time. I think that my associates were a bit unhappy having to do a larger share of the work; however, I put my entire salary into the office pool.

Partly as a result of the malpractice problem, the hospitals had lost a significant amount of money. All of them had also invested a great deal in new equipment, new construction, and larger support staffs after the war. That had created some major debt. The hospitals began to seek partners with which to merge. There were three hospitals in a relatively small area that could have generated a relationship: Presbyterian, Children's, and Mount Zion. Mount Zion and Presbyterian started serious negotiations. It was obvious that if a merger were to be successful, there should be one campus, and Presbyterian had a slightly more developed campus. The real problem developed with consideration of who would be in control. Would the chief of surgery at Mount Zion be willing to cede the title to his counterpart at Presbyterian.? The same problem would be present in every department, The other problem was that Mount Zion was a Jewish institution, and represented a major contribution of the Jewish community to San Francisco. That status was difficult to abandon. After hours of hard work, it was felt that the merger of these two would not work. The situation was reported in Herb Caen's popular column in the San Francisco Chronicle.

"THE FEE ENTERPRISE System: In medical terms, you'd have to say that Presbyterian Hospital is in serious if not critical shape—a $17 million debt and low occupancy, but incredibly good research and surgical facilities in its fortress-like building on Buchanan. Meanwhile, famed Mt. Zion which was losing $100,000 a month a year ago, is now in the black, thanks to the efforts of such as Rhoda (Mrs. Richard) Goldman and Dr. John Kerner, the energetic chief of staff. . . . This is what has led to rumors of a merger of the two facilities, a possibility that, say insiders, 'is far in the future but being discussed.' San Francisco's problem is not unique—too many hospitals, too many overlapping research programs, and no control."

My friend Will Glickman in his usual satiric mode said:

"The enclosed [the above column] raises a matter of some concern within the show-biz community.

"In the event of a merger, which gets top billing? If it becomes Presbyterian-Mt. Zion, I wish to inform you that I will henceforth take my trade elsewhere. If it becomes Mt. Zion-Presbyterian my rabbi will become depressed. If it becomes Zi-Pres or Pres-Zi, please do not be surprised if there is a sudden increase in believers in Faith Healing. [With more joking about a logo] Anxiously, An Old Customer."

As the years went by, a similar problem developed when UCSF Medical Center tried to merge with its counterpart at Stanford. The same problems developed, and the merger was dissolved, with a tremendous loss of money. However, Presbyterian did join with Children's Hospital. That worked, because after a time duplication of services was mostly eliminated.

In spite of the work I was doing, I found time to develop a department strong enough to qualify as a teaching department of obstetrics and gynecology. After a while, it was one of two in California that were not part of a university system. Because of the success of the obstetrical department, the department of pediatrics grew in a remarkable way. It had the first intensive care nursery in San Francisco, and was superior to others, even the UCSF.

When eventually Mount Zion merged with the much larger University of California, the teaching departments merged. The university was anxious to add the Mount Zion intensive care nursery to its own, because it had been a major moneymaker for Mount Zion. I felt that move meant that all obstetrics would have to be transferred to UCSF, since I did not believe Mount Zion could have obstetrics without an intensive care nursery.

Since the university wanted obstetrics and especially the nursery, I felt that the university should move something of equal importance to the Mount Zion campus. The university considered orthopedics and cancer. I was enthusiastic about developing the cancer program, which was one of the weakest at the university. The cancer program was moved to Mount Zion, and it became one of the major cancer centers in the country.

Chapter 14

Karen Smith-McCune

In the 1990s, the fund started by Helen Rowan had grown substantially. The then chairman of the Department of Obstetrics and Gynecology at UCSF, Robert Jaffe, Dean Joe Martin, and Chancellor Julius Krevans suggested that there should be a chair at our medical school bearing my name. I was touched and honored by their suggestion. Of course, it demanded that I come up with $500,000. However, that turned out to be relatively easy, particularly with the support of Mary Jane Brinton and other patients.

There was a university announcement of the professorship, and many nice things were said about me, not the least of which was a statement by Bob Jaffe. "It is fitting that UCSF honor him as a clinician and scholar by establishing this professorship, which will provide a key step in the expansion of cancer research and patient care planned with Mount Zion. John's professional life has been completely dedicated to the university, to Mount Zion, and to the medical community overall."

Then came an unusually graceful gesture on the part of the chancellor. He has, as one of the "perks" of his office, a beautiful old home located above the campus, looking out over the city. It is staffed by a particularly elegant crew. Doctor Krevans stated that he wanted to give a dinner to honor me and the chair. Though since then there have been a number of endowed chairs, at that time there were only a few. The invitation included my privilege to invite those I wanted, up to about forty people. He would invite my professor, Doctor Jaffe, the dean, and others from the university staff. I selected my closest friends and all available family members.

I thought for such an important occasion that I should treat myself to a new suit. I went to Bullock and Jones, the best men's store in San Francisco. They suggested a fine Italian suit. In spite of a number of visits to the tailor, they could not get it to fit well. Finally, they said that they would replace it with an Oxford suit, the top of the line at the time. It fit beautifully. The dinner was a splendid affair, one of the most impressive things that had ever happened to me. There were embarrassingly flattering speeches, and finally one from me. Unfortunately, I do not remember what I said, but I have always felt at ease giving talks. My father insisted that I take public speaking from the time I started high school, and my lessons there did me great service. It was a grand night, and in spite of various other awards, this was special, since it was from the university, not just Mount Zion.

The search for the proper medical school chair took some time, but we finally settled on Karen Smith-McCune. Karen had already done outstanding work in relation to cancer of the cervix, an area in which I had had great interest since my resident days with Herbert Traut. She was particularly unusual, because she was one of those rare individuals who could function in a clinical setting while pursuing outstanding studies as a scientist.

Karen had been the director of the UCSF Dysplasia Clinic since July 1991. She had graduated with a BS in honors biochemistry from McGill University in 1975, then attended the University of Cambridge, where she received a history and philosophy of science diploma in 1976. In 1981, she completed a PhD program at Rockefeller University, and in 1986 received her medical degree from Stanford University. She completed her ob/gyn residency at UCSF in 1990, followed by a postdoctoral fellowship with J. Michael Bishop. He had received a Nobel Prize, and was named chancellor, a professor of microbiology and immunology, and director of the famous Hooper Foundation. Karen was the kind of doctor that Doctor Traut would have wanted me to select. Beside all of that, she was a charming woman, with two lovely daughters and a brilliant scientist husband. She is much involved in community affairs, particularly as relates to education. Her original goal was "to extend the work I had done (along with others), but on a molecular basis, and continue to specifically identify potential markers for diagnosis."

I decided that I should give a dinner honoring the selection of Karen, and booked a particularly attractive room in Stars Restaurant. I invited members of the committee that selected Karen, and invited her husband and Doctor Jaffe as well. Guests also included major supporters of my fund and of our university. I introduced Karen, and Doctor Jaffe had good things to say. Karen spoke in a charming way. The dinner was a huge success. One of the products of that evening was my decision to have annual dinners with speakers on the subject of cancer research, with a guest list that included lay people who were interested in our efforts to cure this group of diseases.

Karen was promoted regularly, and became an associate professor in 2002. She also was rewarded with tenure. She has had many honors nationally and internationally, but the most rewarding thing about her is how much she is liked and admired by students, residents, and colleagues.

Karen has extended our knowledge of causes of cervical cancer, its diagnosis and treatment. She is working now on a much lower-cost method of screening people for the viruses that cause most cervical cancer. Doing smears and colposcopy (a method of looking at the cervix with a special microscope) would only be necessary when a dangerous virus was present. The program would probably save millions of lives, especially in Africa, where cervical cancer is one of the two or three major causes of death in women. For her work, she has received major grants from The National Cancer Institute. In 2003, she took a sabbatical to Paris. From there, she was able to get to Africa to get a firsthand look at the problems there.

I predict an important future for this remarkable woman.

Chapter 15

1999

In February 1999, I had my eightieth birthday. I thought it was time to retire. The economics of medical practice made it impossible for me to stay in practice as a single practitioner, especially since I had not permitted myself to do major surgery for ten years, and even minor surgery for five. I decided that I should discuss my retirement with each patient over a period of one year. I received a flood of letters that were touching. One follows in part:

"M.C.H.

"I am reflecting on your retirement and how privileged I feel to have been your patient for the last 24 years. I have often thought how lucky I was to have been referred to you. I think it was the psychiatrist of some long forgotten boyfriend of mine who recommended that I call you. Since then, you have seen me through many phases of my life, and you have always provided me with the highest possible quality of medical care and the best possible advice.

"I miss you as a physician and as a friend. You are my favorite doctor, and I have always looked forward to my appointments and the opportunity to ask you questions that I have only felt comfortable asking you. You have been unfailingly kind, gracious, and thoughtful, and you have been incredibly generous with your time. I have also loved hearing about your latest trips and gathering travel tips. It has been fun to see the new photographs on your office wall as you continue to explore the world.

"In short, I will miss you greatly, and I do hope that we can stay in touch.

"I am enclosing a check for your foundation in commemoration of your retirement and in appreciation for all the wonderful care you have provided me in the past. There is no way that I can ever thank you enough for all the help you have given me. I owe so much to you—including my children. Thank you so very, very much.

"I would also love to give a party in your honor around November 30.

[Signed]

"Maryellen"

The party was a grand affair. It was given at the top of the Transamerica Pyramid building in San Francisco. It was a crystal clear night with a full moon. The setting was elegant, with seven tables of eight. The guest list included mostly favorite patients and friends. During the course of the evening, there were a number of flattering speeches, but finally it was my turn. I did not read what I had to say, nor did I use notes. However, I had thought about what I should say, and I have the original plan.

Party Talk

"The Yiddish language is replete with words and phrases that have no equivalent in the English language. That being so, many of these words and phrases are included in our vernacular. One of the less familiar but wonderful words is 'nachas.' Classically this word describes the feeling that you get when one of your children does something wonderful, like being elected the president of the student body. Well, I must tell you that I get the same feeling seeing M.C.H. I remember her as young woman considering going into law. She went to Boalt Hall Law School at UC, where she graduated under the guidance of Herma Kay (who is with us this evening). After graduation, she worked her way up to the top of her profession, literally and figuratively, for as a chief legal counsel, her office was at the very top of this building. When she married F., she moved over to The American President Line, where she had an equally impressive position. With all of that, she had time to have two wonderful children at a point in life when most women would decide to continue more along the professional path. She has done a great job as a mom. Finally, she had time to arrange this splendid evening. So, I raise my glass to M.C.H., who has given me so much *nachas*.

"Last year, my accountant said, 'John it's time for you to retire. It's costing you too much to practice.' He wanted me to send letters to my patients announcing my retirement. I just could not get myself to do that. I have known so many people for so long that I felt it would be worthwhile to invest some money in seeing them, helping them to plan future care, and also so that I could say a personal goodbye.

"Well, all of that turned out to be much more difficult for me than I expected. Most of my patients seemed more like friends than patients. So by the end of each day there seemed to be quarter of an inch of tears on the floor of my consultation room. Because of that, I am particularly grateful tonight to get to meet with so many of you, which reminds me that just because I will no longer see you as patients and colleagues does not mean that we cannot meet again. Obviously, in my long professional life, I did a lot of professional things, but I am sure I will remember the people with whom I dealt much longer than I will remember how to do a hysterectomy.

"Besides the practice, I always enjoyed teaching students, residents, colleagues, and anyone else I could get to listen to my talks and to look at my pictures. I particularly remember Morrie Mink as an intern , and here he is a senior in that complicated area which was once just ENT. Also, here is one my residents, Marilyn Milkman, who recently has been a major support.

"People repeatedly ask me what I will do now. You all know that Gwen and I love to travel, and we plan to do as much as we can as long as we can. It will be a lot easier not having to worry about the patients, our children, and even our home. For we are in the process of moving to smaller and more easily managed digs. I like games. Golf is only good a couple of days a week. I like table games like dominoes, chess, and the Japanese game of Go, but you can only do so much of that. I want much to try my hand at writing. There is plenty of inspiration here in Alice Adams, Carol Field, Georgia Hesse, and Merla Zellerbach. I have some paints; I'd like to get them out and try again. Probably more important, I hope to continue to be involved in the UC/Mount Zion cancer program in which I have been much concerned since its inception, There are also serious plans to construct a women's health care center to care for women from teenagers to the post-menopausal, with all the facilities needed, including mammography, ambulatory surgery, lectures, and hopefully obstetrics. We already have the people. We only need the building, and I think that can be managed under the leadership of Gene Washington, Ernie Ring, and Elena Gates. So, I do not plan to fade away.

"Finally, I would like to leave you with some good advice. Exercise regularly. With apologies to Herman, I believe it is good for your heart and bones. Further, there seems to be less breast cancer among women who exercise regularly. My experience is that it is also psychotherapeutic. Here I must defer to Bob Wallerstein and Carroll Brodsky. I think there is a real value in getting proper vitamins. Of course, you can get that with five different fruits and vegetables daily. But, if you don't have such a diet, be sure to get 500 mg of vitamin C, 400 Units of E, and about one mg of folic acid, and some calcium. C and E clearly seem to be associated with a lower incidence of all cancers, and I believe that folic acid is probably good for hearts. (Again, with apologies to Herman.) I also think that daily low-dose aspirin helps protect against heart attacks and colon cancer.

"Now again, I must thank Maryellen and Frank for bringing us together on this wonderful evening."

It is interesting to see how all of my wishes turned out. The games took up less of my time, mostly because the people I played golf and other games with were dying off rapidly. I never got the paints out. I did write a book, *Combat Medic, World War II*, about which more later. I also have had a part in developing a new anticancer drug. I plan to give more information about that too. The Comprehensive Women's Health Center has been established in the old Cancer Center Building, which was once the Mount Zion Pavilion, and before that Maimonides Hospital. The center is splendid, and represents a great architectural achievement. I also have found myself involved in the finding of a new head of the gynecological cancer program.

One of the unexpected pleasures of my retiring has been that I was now in a position where I could socialize with patients whom I had known only in the office environment, and with whom such association might not been appropriate while I was in practice. Two days a week, I arranged to have lunch with former patients and other persons for whom I had not formerly had time. I had the opportunity to get to know better many of the faculty members of the Department of Obstetrics and

Gynecology at UCSF. I have luncheons where I can work out strategies for our cancer research program. There was time now to work on my first book, *Combat Medic*, and to meet with publishers, editors, and others of special interest. What a great dividend I gained from retiring.

Chapter 16

Letters

During World War II, I wrote over 200 letters to my mother, my father, and my sister. They were saved and returned to me after I returned home. I had been serving in a combat infantry division, The 35th. I had been, among other things, a battalion surgeon, the most forward position in which a doctor could be placed. The job of the battalion aid group was to pick up the wounded and try to get them in good enough condition to be evacuated, and to protect them from being wounded again. Doctors are no longer used for that purpose. Too many were killed or wounded. The letters I wrote remained in my possession, but not reviewed until I got close to retirement. One day, almost fifty years later, I got the letters out. I decided that it would be fun to write something making use of the information they contained. I began to write in sequence. At first, I thought I might write a novel, but soon found that I did not have the skills for that modality, so I decided that I should write a memoir, which would give me maximum use of the letters, and some freedom beyond that of an autobiography. I wrote three or four chapters that I worked on during breaks in my day, as I approached the time I had set for retiring.

One of the things that I did in preparation for retiring was to discuss with each of my patients where they should go for continued care. I had allowed a year to carry out that plan. One day, Karen W. came for a routine check. I had delivered her only child, and I had treated her after that for a number of years. She had had experience as an editor. She, like so many others, asked me what I planned to do when I retired. I stated that I loved to travel, as did my wife, that I enjoyed games like chess, the Japanese game of Go, dominoes, and golf. I also stated that I thought I would like to try my hand at writing, since I had enjoyed doing it when I was a premedical student in Berkeley, where I had a minor in English. She asked me if I had written anything recently, and I said I had, but that I did not have anything I was ready to let others read. She finally persuaded me to let her see what I had written to date. I was not easy to persuade, but she reminded me of her qualifications, and I figured I had nothing to lose. So I gave her what I had written to that date. The next day, she called me to say that she was moved by what I had written, and that I had to continue with the project. Further, she stated she would be pleased to help me with editing. I agreed and decided that I would continue on the project.

When I actually retired, I had more time, and each day I tried to write something. I enrolled in a writing class at the Fromm Institute, where I picked up some good ideas. Periodically, I would send a chapter or two to Karen, until at long last after a year, the book was complete.

I then had the chore of finding a publisher or an agent or a combination. Though Karen and others who had helped me with my efforts thought the book was good, I could not find an agent or a publisher. I sent copies of the manuscript to innumerable people, many of whom wrote back pleasant letters, but declined to represent me or to publish. Finally, one day after a dominoes game, I discussed the problem with my friend Don Sweet, who said I should call a friend of his who had recently had a book published by a publisher in Berkeley. I got in touch with that publisher, who agreed to see me and to review my book. He read what I had written and agreed to publish it if I would invest some money. The amount of money was not great, and I decided that I should take the offer. He wrote a contract, and I had it reviewed by a lawyer friend who had himself been a successful author. The publisher hired an editor who was excellent. He did not change much, but his suggestions were good.

The publisher sent me a proposed cover for the book. It looked good to me. Essentially, it made use of a picture of the medals I had earned during the war. I showed the cover to members of my family. My older son's wife and daughter are talented artistically. They suggested changes in color and lettering, but my second son and his wife felt that their son, Ryan, could do a better overall cover. He sent me his suggestion, which was different. Essentially, the background was of an aid man administering an IV to a wounded soldier. This was framed by the various medals and awards I had received, including the highly valued

Combat Medical Badge. That badge was worn only by soldiers who worked with the most forward troops. The medals included a Bronze Star with Oak Leaf Cluster; the European Theater Ribbon with a silver star, which is the equivalent of five battle stars; and a few others not as important. There was also a Presidential Citation ribbon. I asked Ryan to make a few minor changes, which he did promptly. It is amazing what can be done when the whole cover is on a computer disc. When I showed Ryan's cover to the publisher, he accepted it immediately, even though he had already paid the artist for the first cover. The publisher thought that it was particularly charming that the cover of the book would be done by my grandson, to whom he sent a check.

One of my favorite patients, Maryellen, having heard of the book, offered to give a book-signing party when the book was completed. It was she who gave me the splendid party when I retired. We set the date some months ahead. Though the publisher agreed on the date, I became increasingly restless as the time grew closer, because I had yet to see the finished product. In the meantime, the publisher had announcement cards printed, with the invitation printed on them. The card, like a postcard, had the cover of the book reproduced on one side, with the invitation on the reverse side. They looked great. The book-signing was to be a cocktail party in the room at the top of the Transamerica Pyramid in San Francisco, where my retirement party had been held.

I got my first look at the completed book on the day of the party. It looked good to me, especially since I was worried that the book might not be finished in time.

The party was splendid. The setting was magnificent. Again from the windows there was the perfect panoramic view of the Bay Area. There were tables around for those who wished to sit. I had had two posters made. They too reproduced the cover of the book, and were placed by the entrance. On one side of the room, there was a long table, with a pile of books on one end, and a setup for a bookstore representative on the other. I was to sit behind the table and sign books until it was time to talk.

For the occasion, I got out my old dress uniform. It was like new because I hardly ever wore it during the war. In combat, I wore clothes that were supplied to infantrymen; though I often wore my officer's bars.

In addition, before I went overseas and after the war, most cities did not require dress uniforms, but required only a dress shirt and slacks. So, there was even less wear than expected on my dress uniform. Interestingly, I could still get into the uniform, though it was slightly snug around the waist. The fact that I fit in the uniform was a constant source of comment by the guests. We were limited by the fire marshals to one hundred people, including employees. That made selection of the guest list difficult. In retrospect, I am sure that some people were not pleased with being left out. Though our host had arranged to take care of parking, some of the attendants apparently did not know that. The price of the garage was high, and a small number did not use the garage, which was sad, since it would have been easier. One couple left, which was especially upsetting. They missed a wonderful evening.

The food was superb, and there was unlimited wine.

Finally, it was time for speeches. Maryellen, in her usual gracious fashion, welcomed everyone. The publisher was next. He talked too long, and about other things he was publishing, though he said nice things about me and my book. Finally, it was my turn. I gave what was to turn out to be my "stump speech." I told a bit about how I came to write the book, and about those who encouraged and helped me. I read three passages, with some explanation for each. I finished by telling the rest of the story, which ended with my return home and finding my future wife.

We sold a good number of books. It was a great night, and made the effort involved in writing and producing *Combat Medic, World War II* worth it.

The second reading of my book was at the Monticello Hotel, in a lovely room called The Library, furnished with comfortable chairs, and a setup of wine and cheese. I appeared again in full dress uniform, complete with decorations and various insignia. I had sent out a number of invitations to old patients who could not come to my first reading because of lack of space. Also, because this sort of reading was a regular event at The Monticello, there were people present whom I did not know. I did the same talk this time, probably better, because I had done it before. Again, we sold more books than expected, and we ran out. I even contributed one that I had brought for myself. The audience was first-rate, which made the evening even better, with a wonderful feeling.

Among those who came was an patient who was at the time a police lieutenant. Shortly after the reading, the police officer's mother sent me a copy of the San Francisco police newspaper that contained an ad for a tour of the battlefields of Europe. The trip was to start in Normandy, with visits to the landing beaches and museums, to go on to Bastogne, across the Rhine near Koblentz, then go down the Rhine, following the course of the 101st Airborne Division.

I talked with the agent who had organized the tour, mentioned my book, and indicated interest. The next day the agent, who incidentally had a wonderful Irish accent, called my wife from Ireland. She said that her husband said she had to get me and my wife to join their tour. She said that he threatened her with something terrible if we did not come. She offered us a significant reduction in what already was a low-cost trip. Gwen and I agreed to go. We decided that we would go to Paris a few days early, and then join the group, which planned a brief tour of Paris, and a first night in Creully, near Caen.

In the meantime, I did a similar presentation at Books Inc., a neighborhood bookstore. People I knew in the neighborhood came. The best of the many bookstores that I spoke at was Book Passage in Marin County. This had a large attendance, mostly of old patients. The publicity was good. The room was full, with people standing around the edges and in the rear.

I did a short TV interview in Santa Rosa, a long radio show in Inverness, and an interesting radio interview in Santa Cruz, where we stayed the night. I never knew whether these shows resulted in significant sales, but they were fun to do.

I found that my infantry division, The 35th, had a newspaper, The 35th Divisionnaire, which gave it considerable publicity, as did our local Nob Hill Gazette and the San Francisco Chronicle. I received complimentary letters, as well as other related information, from sources all over the country. Some of the people I knew, but there were many I had never heard of. I had sent copies to various people for reviews, some of which were on the back cover of the book. People were impressed with particularly pleasant comments by California Senator Dianne Feinstein, the editor of the Nob Hill Gazette, Merla Zellerbach, and my English professor.

Our battlefield trip started on May 14, 2003. Gwen and I went to the Hotel Royal Saint-Honoré on the suggestion of another ex-patient. It had a lovely location on the Rue Saint-Honoré, close to the Place Vendôme. We had a fine visit, with food in favorite restaurants, including La Coupole and Apicius, which deserves its two stars. In Paris, we found some wonderful exhibits: On our first day we walked to The Louvre, where there was a show of "Michel-Ange" (Michelangelo). There was a show of Dufy at the Maillol Museum, which revealed him to be much more versatile than I expected. These were topped by an extensive show of the work of Magritte at The Jeu de Palme.

On the day we were to meet the group, instead of our going to the airport, they agreed to pick us up on their arrival. The group had shrunk significantly from the original thirty. When the war with Iraq started, half of those planning to come canceled. Then, with a weakened economy and the advent of SARS (a contagious upper respiratory infection), there were further cancellations. That left our group with eight tourists and a guide. That made it possible for us to travel in a van that held nine people and their luggage. It turned out to be an excellent German vehicle. That group arrived at our hotel a bit earlier than we expected. We immediately noted that they were all young by our standards. Everyone seemed pleased to meet us. They knew about my book, which all but one had read. They rapidly added our luggage (two fairly small suitcases) and us, and we were off.

Since most of the group had never been to Paris, the tour guide, David Harper, set off to hit some of the high spots. He was charming, and we soon found that he spoke excellent French, American English, and superb German. The members of the group all turned out to be involved with police work. The woman who organized the trip was married to Danny Lopez, police captain of the Police Patrol Boat of San Francisco. She was from Ireland, and had retained a pure Irish accent and vocabulary. There was a couple from Bishop, California. Paul Kenney was a retired highway patrol officer, but still young enough to be my child. His wife, Karen, was an attractive, enthusiastic blonde. There were two single officers: Jo Cordes, was on the sexual assault detail of the San Francisco Police Department, and Bob Lee, on the fraud detail. Jo had studied World War II, and had a never-ending list of questions, though he tried to limit himself. Bob was very quiet, but obviously interested in everything.

We drove about the city, getting the best possible views of structures like the Opera, the Eiffel Tower, and Sacré Cœur. We stopped for lunch in the Montmartre. It was Sunday; the place was jammed and the prices outrageous, but the area has its charms, and the group took it all in graciously. Then we were on our way to Normandy.

Gwen and I were worried that we would arrive in Normandy late in the day. We were surprised that our vehicle was able to travel at a faster speed than we expected. So we arrived in Creully much earlier than we expected. The hotel Hostellerie Saint Martin was very old, probably close to 500 years old, but it had been maintained beautifully. The hotel had just twelve rooms, so it was fortunate that our group was small. Our room was up a tower spiral staircase. It had a large bedroom and a second smaller room, plus a nice bathroom, and a separate room for the toilet. There was plenty of space, welcome after our smaller, though more modern, room in Paris.

At dinner, over wine, we got to know each other, and the vibes were good. The dining room was of moderate size. It had a vaulted ceiling that had been freshly painted. The table linens were of white and pink, and the setting was elegant for so small an establishment. The meal was excellent, with superb local seafood and more good wine. At dessert time, Andree Chan came to our table to introduce herself as the vice president of 35th "Santa Fe" Division in Normandy. She was wearing a pin that bore the insignia of the division. The group, whose president is Guy Latour, honors my division for liberating a number of towns in Normandy, especially Gieville of which M. Latour is mayor. Mme. Chan showed me part of her collection of memorabilia of the 35th. She invited me and the members of my group to a lunch two days later.

For the next two days, we toured the landing beaches and the museums that had pictures and memorabilia of June 6, 1944. Everywhere, I was greeted graciously, because it became known that I had served in combat in Normandy. The museum directors presented me with diplomas, medals, and free admission. Of course, members of my group were interested in details and the films. They often asked me questions, which I enjoyed answering.

With the money saved from my admission charges, David bought me a bottle of Calvados. The group helped me to finish the bottle, developing a taste for that liquor, for which I had fond memories.

I wore a dress uniform shirt I had with me. It had on it my various decorations that I had worn when my book was first introduced, plus a couple of more minor ones. It was an impressive array.

On the morning of the luncheon, after visiting Omaha Beach, we went to the American Cemetery. It was magnificently designed. At one end is a monument to the various units that were involved in the invasion. The walls showed the progress of the Allied forces. I was pleased to find an array of fresh flowers near a statue in the center of the monument. At the far end of the graveyard, past the rows of crosses and Stars of David, was the chapel. I had been there before, and was touched by being there, and by the tasteful design. I found myself fighting back tears as I thought of the many fine men we had lost in that invasion. At the end of our tour of the Omaha area, we were at the far end of the beach at Pointe du Hoc. There we were met by a small delegation from our host group, Santa Fe Division in Normandy. They escorted us to the site of the luncheon, which was the small hotel owned by the president, M. Latour, Motel du Bocage in Gieville. Outside, we were met by a large group of members. They all wore pins bearing the insignia of the 35th Division. There was much talk about the fact that I was looking for the baby I had delivered during the battle for Mortain. The baby now would be 59. Her mother had been brought to my aid station carried on a ladder padded with a quilt. The baby had presented as a footling breech. That story had been in the local newspapers, which was how these people knew I was coming. Among the people in the group was a couple that had come from Nancy, about 300 miles away. The setting was lovely. The owner was particularly proud of the colorful flowers growing in profusion. Finally, we went in to lunch. There was a display table with some information about the 35th and some clippings about me from the newspaper Ouest France. There was a banquet table magnificently set for twenty-four people. The first course, already on the table, was a melon containing a red liqueur in a lovely tulip glass. The luncheon started with champagne and a welcoming speech. I was made an honorary member of their organization, and I was called upon to speak at that juncture. The generosity of the occasion, combined with the morning visit to the cemetery, was almost more than I could handle. I usually find it easy to talk in public, but on this occasion I had to fight back the tears. I did manage a "thank you." The luncheon was various dishes from Normandy, with good red and white wines. After dessert, there were more speeches and more gifts. I was given a splendid bottle of Calvados. People who had read my book knew how I had treasured that liquor. I received a cap bearing the insignia of the group, and a container of sand from Omaha Beach. There also was a medal honoring my division. After lunch, we were taken to a small museum that the president had stocked with all sorts of equipment and memorabilia of the 35th. We then went to a nearby small church that had once been a part of a leper home, The Memorial de la Madeleine, that had been converted to be a tribute to the 29th and the 35th divisions in 1994. The walls were decorated with flags of the divisions and other memorabilia, and there were plaques in honor of those who had died. It was done with great taste.

We finally headed to our hotel, having had an unforgettable experience. That evening, two reporters came to have dinner with Gwen and me at our hotel in Creully. They took excellent pictures that were e-mailed to me. The pictures were used in two long articles in Ouest France about me and my quest to find the "baby." These resulted in a large number of e-mails to me. Interestingly, they all offered thanks to my division, and offered to try to help me in my search for the baby I delivered during the war.

After this splendid introduction to World War II sites, we headed out for Bastogne. By this time, our group began treating me with gentle courtesy. For instance, they insisted that Gwen and I sit up in front with the driver, which was particularly appreciated by Gwen. Our destination for the day was a small hotel, L'Horizon, in Thionville, in northeastern France. It was chosen because it was close to the city of Bastogne, and because it is elegant. It was a long drive from Normandy, so we made two breaks. The freeways in France have first-rate rest stops, with small, well-stocked markets, cafeteria-style restaurants, newsstands, and other conveniences that travelers might want. After one such stop, we found that we had made better time than we expected, so we could stop at Rheims, which was slightly off our route. The cathedral, as is well-known, is one of the grandest in the world, and the light was just right to set the rose window ablaze. For me, the great places of worship—

whether they be church, synagogue, or mosque—inspire awe, and certainly bring God to mind. We had coffee in a charming, old, but well-maintained, bar near the cathedral, and were on our way to L'Horizon.

The hotel was far superior to anything we had anticipated. Because our group was small, we could be put up in such a place, rather than a more commercial establishment. The setting was charming, with most rooms looking over a terrace bordered with flowers in full bloom. Beyond the terrace was a valley that extended to the horizon.

Our room faced that view. It was large and furnished in simple but tasteful style. The bathroom was modern, with two sinks, a bathtub, and shower, with a separate room for the toilet.

After we were settled, I went for a short walk in the neighborhood. This was a residential area; the homes were well-maintained, and were of a Mediterranean style—surprising, in that we were in Lorraine, which borders on Germany and Luxembourg, as well as Belgium. Before dinner on the terrace, we were treated to champagne from the owner. The dining room was well-furnished, with a pink tablecloth on a large table provided for our group. Dinner was followed by talk in the lounge, fueled by the fine Calvados I had brought from Normandy. Gwen and I were ready for bed, while the rest continued.

On the following morning, we headed for Bastogne and the American Cemetery and Monument just out of town.

The cemetery, like that in Normandy, was touching, to say the least. The battle in that area was probably the worst that we Americans had to fight, and there were many casualties. The war in Iraq was going on, and the cemetery reminded us that war is not a game. At the entrance to the cemetery was the simple grave of George Patton, certainly the best of our field generals. It had a cross, like the graves of so many of the soldiers, and the inscription of rank and years of his life. The only special thing about it was that the grave was separate, surrounded by a white chain. But there he lay at the head of the troops of whom he was so proud. The cemetery is over fifty acres, and is surrounded by a variety of trees. There are well over 5,000 men and one woman buried here.

The entrance gates were impressive, and each gate had a golden wreath, such as those we had on our sleeves awarded for valor. There were massive pillars supporting the gates. The memorial was a tall, columnar structure. There was a simple carillon in it, and a small chapel at its base. On one side there are maps illustrating the actions of the various divisions involved in the Battle of the Bulge. The other side had a list of missing men involved in the battle. In the chapel was the seal of the United States, and below it was the inscription:

1941-1945
IN PROUD REMEMBRANCE OF THE ACHIEVEMENTS OF HER SONS AND IN HUMBLE TRIBUTE TO THEIR SACRIFICES THIS MEMORIAL HAS BEEN ERECTED BY THE UNITED STATES OF AMERICA.

Above the entrance to the chapel was a massive sculpture of the Angel of Peace. Above her was a dove. To either side, as one approached the cemetery itself, were two large maps, one showing the progress of the war in the west, and the other showing the course of the Battle of the Bulge.

Nearby was the monument, a double circle of columns, each bearing the name of units involved in the battle. The symbol of my 35th Infantry was conspicuously emblazoned on one of the columns.

We then toured the area where the fighting took place, and experienced how difficult the terrain must have been. Finally, we went into the city. We had lunch in a small cafe on the town square. We then searched for the location of the site of the aid station I had set up in the middle of the battle. I had chosen a portion of the railroad station, because there was running water, and I could heat the area with a stove that I had had tied to my three-quarter-ton truck. We found the exact site because the original, beat-up sign, BASTOGNE SUD, is still there. I had photographed it during the war. The station is in the process of being repaired, since it had been badly damaged by shell fire. It is to be a bus station. My triumphant picture was taken there. That evening at dinner, for the last time, I put on the uniform I had brought along. The next day we were heading for Germany. On the way, we stopped to see the fortifications of Guentrange, a major portion of the Maginot Line. These fortifications were amazing in their complexity, with habitation for over 400 soldiers beneath tremendous fortifications. Of course, in

World War II, the Germans went around the Maginot Line through Belgium, so all of that work was to no avail.

I have had ambivalent feelings whenever entering Germany. Around the time of our invasion of Normandy, I had begun to be aware of the mistreatment of Jews by The Reich. Actually, the atrocities were even worse than I imagined. In combat in Normandy, at nighttime, we often could hear the German soldiers talking just beyond our lines. There is no question that I feared being captured more than being wounded or even killed. This fear was accentuated by the fact that I was put in command of a battalion aid station, with no real background for such a command. On one occasion in the nighttime, I was moving my unit to a position to be able to support the combat infantry the next day. Along the road I had selected, my unit was stopped by a soldier who came out of his foxhole. He asked where I was going, and I said that I was planning to set up an aid station. He said, "If you go down this road another hundred yards, you will be setting up for the Krauts." I still have nightmares about that event. Obviously, I turned around. I am aware that there is a new generation of Germans, but the sound of the language still has unpleasant associations.

We started our tour through Germany on a boat trip up the Rhine, starting just below Koblentz. Our plan was to follow the course taken by the 101st Airborne Division. It's history had been revived in a television series, "The Band of Brothers," and was therefore a logical route for our group to take. We traveled on the Rhine in a large, comfortable, cruise riverboat. There were few travelers. The tourist business had suffered greatly because of the war in Iraq and the poor economy in the United States. That in no way affected the scenery, which was enchanting. This portion of the Rhine has lovely small towns, invariably with old castles protecting them on high hills above. Our first stop was Rittenburg. It was a small city, but it held our first look at typical, well-preserved Bavarian architecture. There was one narrow street with restaurants on both sides where there was music and a good deal of beer drinking. Our group enjoyed the atmosphere. We were welcome, especially since tourism in the area was off forty percent. This was one of our rare one-night stops.

Our route then took us through Rothenburg, Heidelberg, and Nuremberg. The architecture of Rothenburg was particularly interesting, with the various gates cut under tall towers often bearing a clock. The buildings dated from about 1250, so the styles varied from Gothic through the Renaissance period. But together, these structures presented a charming whole. The view of Heidelberg from its castle were impressive. Nuremberg, which of course was the epicenter of Nazism, had an impressive building. It was the unfinished headquarters of the Nazi Party. It was in the shape of a huge horseshoe, and contained a museum featuring the history of Nazism. The major group of visitors was schoolchildren. We felt that it was right that the students were shown not only the successes of the Nazis, but the terrible things that they did. The museum was well-organized, with films, recordings, pictures, and various memorabilia. Later on, we had a similar experience in visiting Dachau, a concentration camp for Jews and others not favored by the Nazis, who were first in forced labor, but then slaughtered in large numbers. Here too students were being led by their teachers through the grim museum. Eventually we traveled through Munich to Berchtesgaden. Of course, in Munich we had a typical lunch of sausages, sauerkraut and beer in one of the major beer halls.

Our final stop was in the lovely city of Berchtesgaden. Our small hotel was on a hill on the edge of the small city. Our room had a large balcony looking out over a splendid, unspoiled valley surrounded by the snow-capped mountains of the Bavarian Alps. Off far to the left was a small village nestled in a valley. Here we were greeted effusively, since we were the first American tourists seen that year. The meals here were elegant and though German, were not heavy as we had expected. The German beer was great.

We remained in this beautiful area for a few days. On our first morning we took a trip to the Eagle's Nest (Kehlsteinhaus), the place where Hitler entertained his important guests. We learned that he never slept there, that he had a home below, as did many of the top Nazis. The road that went up toward the Eagle's Nest was a feat of engineering, having been blasted out of solid rock at great expense to the government. From the parking lot, reached by special buses, there is a huge, brass-lined elevator that took us the rest of the way, 407 feet up. The Nest is a spacious building that has one large reception room and one smaller one. The views are spectacular of Berchtesgadener Land.

Hitler used this place rarely, and in retrospect, it was a spectacular waste of money.

The next day, we went to a salt mine, of all things. The mine had been there for centuries, so its galleries extended for miles underground. We all had to put on miner's clothing, which resembled heavy scrub suits. We rode into the mines on a small train. We passed numerous galleries. Eventually we arrived at a place where supplies were sent to a lower level down a slide. This slide was offered to us. It looked frightening, but David convinced me and Gwen that we should go first. Being careful to keep our feet up so as not to have them stop us, we clung on to each other and made the descent without incident, even though it was long and steep. That, of course, shamed the others, so they followed us down. The last part of the visit was on a barge that passed over a large underground lake. Ore was mined and dumped into the lake after crushing, and the salt settled out. It was in this mine and other similar ones in the area where much of the Nazi loot was stored. The salt was the source of wealth for the rulers of this area.

Nearby was a lovely large lake, which was pollution-free. There was limited, controlled fishing. All boats were electric. There was a charming church, and next to it was a simple restaurant, which served local fare.

We ended our tour in Salzburg, which had sustained some damage in the war because many of the elite German troops were garrisoned there. It was a beautiful city, also built with the wealth brought to the church from the sale of salt. The Bishop's palace was especially splendid because of its position looking down on the city, and because of the rich decoration over many of the doorways, as well as the splendid porcelain stoves placed to provide heat. It is a tourist center, but there were few tourists at that time.

Finally, after our last dinner, David brought out his guitar, which he brought from his home close by. We had had no room for it in our crowded vehicle. When he got around to singing French cafe songs, he had the women swooning. We had him going for hours. It was a perfect ending for our trip. We exchanged gifts. Mine was a copy of my book, *Combat Medic, World War II*, for those who did not have one.

This pleasant group continued to look after me and Gwen. Even at the airport in San Francisco, someone grabbed our suitcases and put them on a cart. What a wonderful trip!

When I returned home I found that the book was doing well, so an ex-patient, Rosemarie, offered to "clean up" the first addition and make a few small additions, including more illustrations. I had been getting regular royalties, which were greater than I had expected. Suddenly, I stopped hearing from the publisher. I got no statements and no money for about six months. I wrote repeatedly, but got no good answers. Even the lawyer who helped me with the contract could only get me a record of sales, but no money. At this point, I heard from another author, who told me that there was a significant number of authors whose work was supposed to be published without any evidence that that action was taking place—of special concern, because each of them had invested money in his or her project. They wanted to sue. I said that though I was sure that I had money coming, I was not about to sue. I had had too much pleasure from the book. I had had the chance to see many of my old patients, and I had some interesting interviews. I had received significant royalties, which most of the authors had not. Of course, the book led to my wonderful trip to the battlefields of Europe. I thought it would be wise to pick up remaining books, but I could not get through to the publisher or his staff. My brother suggested that we drop by the publishing building. There was a sign on the door stating that they were closed, but my brother encouraged me to knock on the door. To my surprise, there were people there. First, they gave me the remaining copies of my book. The number was small, which was why we had planned a second edition. The publisher was there; he apologetically stated he was broke. He found a good deal of my material, including the disc which contained the new edition. Unfortunately, some of the material was missing. He also had made, then and there, a disc of the first edition. That was about all I could expect.

Within a couple of days, I got a call from Carol Fox, who is director of public relations for UCSF. She wanted to know if I would be a part of an "Evening with the Author" series. I agreed. The interviewer would be Michael Krasny, who is a favorite with locals on one of our local public television stations. But there was an immediate problem. Where could we get the books to sell at the event? Usually, one of the bookstores carries out that task. But there were no books available from the publisher, except the few I had. My wife, Gwen, made the suggestion that I should check with the gift store on the Mount Zion Campus of UCSF. They had purchased 200–300 copies of my books for an event in my honor. They still had a good many copies left. So, I arranged that they sell books at the author event. Thus, they could provide books, turn their inventory into cash, and be able to add money to the good works they support. They were ecstatic. So was I.

The chairman of the program asked me for various materials, including a biography, copies of the book, photographs to be made into slides, and a list of people I wanted notified. I delivered all the material promptly. Since I was going out of town for a much-needed vacation, I checked to be sure that all was in order, for the event was to be only a few days after my return. When I got back to San Francisco, to my dismay, I found that all of my material, even including a poster, had been lost. The slides had not been made. I was particularly upset at the loss of the pictures, which were digitally enhanced copies of those I took during World War II. They had been quite expensive to produce. The invitations had not been sent. At home, all I had were a couple of duplicate slides. Obviously, I had to make the best of the situation. I began to wonder if I had been right to refuse the stipend that had been offered.

In spite of all the problems, the evening was a huge success, even though my guest list had been lost along with most of my slides. There was the general university publicity for the evening. The program was to last an hour and forty-five minutes. I wondered how we could fill that time. I appeared well on time in full uniform. Mr. Krasny was well-prepared. He had read my book, and also some biographical material. He was a superb interviewer. He picked out important parts of my book and of my life to talk about. Most important—without seeming to try, he put me at ease. The audience was with us all the way. It was the best thing of this sort that I had done. I had been on two radio programs and one short TV program, and had held numerous readings in bookstores and other venues. However, this was the most successful presentation I had made.

* * *

There was yet another activity resulting from the book. I had discovered that there was an organization that honors those who served in the Battle of the Bulge. It even has a newspaper. Since I was involved in that battle, I sent a copy of my book to the president of the organization. He invited me to a meeting, which I could not make, but I did get to an annual event that honors those who were in the battle, the largest in U.S. history. There is a plaque on a rock looking over the ocean at Fort Miley where the San Francisco VA Medical Center is located. There, on December 16, the anniversary date of the beginning of the battle, the few survivors and their families assembled. There were wreaths from the Belgians and the Luxembourgers, whose representatives were there. It was a lovely, simple occasion. Flags were flying. The audience looked over the ocean as they heard brief tributes. Again, I was moved almost to tears as I thought of all those who were lost in that great battle, and who therefore did not get to live out their lives, as I have had the good fortune to do. At this affair, the president of the organization asked me to speak at a meeting in about six weeks, which I agreed to do.

The appointed day was a Saturday in March. The weather was unseasonably warm, so I decided to wear my dress uniform shirt with decorations rather than my dress uniform, which would be uncomfortably warm. A former president of the organization had arranged to pick me up. With him was his wife, who was also involved with The Veterans of the Battle of the Bulge, and organization dedicated to those who fought that battle during the winter of 1944–45. Also along was a good friend of theirs, the husband of an old patient of mine who had died recently. I had delivered their three children, and was particularly fond of his wife. She had faced breast cancer at an early age, and had the courage to get pregnant after that diagnosis, even though she had been advised against it. We arrived at the place where the meeting was to be held, a famous fish restaurant in Berkeley. The room was set with tables for around sixty people. The group was interesting. Many of the men had been with the 101st Airborne, which had been surrounded at Bastogne when the Germans almost cut the Allied armies in two. However, the 101st held out until help arrived. A good number of the guests were with the troops that came to their relief, which

included me. We had a nice luncheon, some business, and then it was
my turn to speak.

It was my plan to give special emphasis to my involvement in
the Battle of the Bulge. I started with my background—being called to
duty from an internship on the day before Christmas 1944, with orders
to leave for Army camp in Pennsylvania on the day after Christmas. I
talked a bit about my early experiences, and especially about my stay
with the ski troops of the 10th Mountain Division. I talked briefly about
my being transferred to a combat infantry division that was to take part
in the invasion of Europe. We were shipped by convoy to England. I
recalled when we as invasion troops were reviewed by Churchill,
Eisenhower, and Patton. As they passed through the ranks, Churchill
and Eisenhower would stop occasionally to talk with a soldier. Patton did
not talk. Eisenhower stopped before me and asked,"Where are you from,
Lieutenant?" I replied, "San Francisco, sir." He said, "I really enjoyed
San Francisco. I was stationed at the Presidio. Good luck, soldier."
"Thank you sir." We got to Normandy not long after D-Day. I related
how I became a combat medic. I told of my first experience at being
fired at with mortars, and of one of my brave privates, who remained
standing holding a bottle of plasma connected to a severely wounded
man while the barrage went on. He had a profound influence on me and
my attitude. There were a number of women present—wives and nurses.
So, I recounted how I had delivered a baby presenting as a footling
breech during he Battle of Mortain. Then I related an episode where
my driver, "Gangster" (he had driven for rumrunners in New Jersey
before the war) and I drove our jeep through the German lines to bring
medical supplies to a surrounded battalion during the battle for Mortain.
I spent little time talking about the race across France, when we thought
the war would be over well before Christmas. Then I got to the main
portion of how we thought we would get a chance to regroup over
Christmas, but instead were sent to relieve the surrounded 101st at
Bastogne. En route, I was threatened with court-martial because I would
not send men with severe frostbite back to duty. My most important
effort in that battle was to take two men and as many medical supplies
as we could load on the outside of a tank, and fight our way into
Bastogne, where they were woefully short of medical personnel and
supplies. I only found out at this event that the shortage was because

the major medical unit of the 101st had been captured. I spent the rest of the time talking about the terrible winter fighting, the crossing of the Rhine, the rush of my unit to meet the Russians, the end of the war, occupation, plans to go for the invasion of Japan, and, finally, my lucky return home.

I had planned to read some from my book, but the room was darkened for the few slides I had brought, so I just talked. After the talk, which was received with extensive applause, I remained for an hour or so. Everyone wanted to talk about their experiences in relation to mine, and ask questions. I had brought some books along. The were all sold, and I took home requests for more. I did not expect that.

This was a remarkable group of men. I was the only one who had been an officer. In their units, few officers had survived the battle. They were good men who, like me, hated war. They knew what it was like.

Chapter 17

Search for the "Baby"

During World War II, one of the most dramatic events for me was when I delivered a baby during the major battle for Mortain, during which the Third Army broke through the German lines and crossed France from Normandy. That event is included in the book I wrote about those times, *Combat Medic*.

Parts of the chapter follow:

"On our next move I set up my aid station in back of a partially ruined stone barn, [and] made a crude shelter out of two pup tents. At dusk on our first night in this new location, two Frenchmen came into our station, carrying a ladder. On it, lying on a quilt, was a young woman with a distended abdomen and obviously in active labor. She was in great distress, because of fear and her labor contractions. There was no question that labor was far advanced. I took the young woman to our shelter for further examination. I could barely get into the tent with an aid man, the ladder, and the patient. I put a blanket on the ground and we moved her onto it. It was then necessary to remove our patient's underclothing and she seemed embarrassed. By good fortune, the aid man spoke a little French, so he helped in giving the girl instructions.

"I covered her with one of our blankets and looked at her perineum. With contractions, her labia separated and to my surprise I found that the baby was presenting as a footling breech. I could see its buttocks and one foot. Under best of conditions, breech deliveries, particularly of first babies, are of major concern to obstetricians. The largest part of the baby, the head and shoulders, comes last. In this case a presenting foot complicated matters. Cesarean section was out of the question, and also there was not time enough to get this woman to a hospital.

"I had to get more help. Inside the tent were two aid men, the patient, and me. We took up all available space.

"Naturally I did not have obstetrical forceps, which are often used on the aftercoming head. I washed my hands as best I could. I did not have sterile gloves. I delivered the baby, using a complicated maneuver that I had learned as an obstetrical intern. The baby, a girl, was fine.

"Just before the mother had been brought to our station, the ambulance assigned to us from the collecting company had left with two badly wounded men, and it returned at this point. Occasionally we heard the tearing sound of German hand-held rapid fire weapons. Our men called them burp guns. There was some responding fire from our side. In spite of that we loaded mother and baby into the ambulance. We also loaded the two men who came with her. I encouraged the mother to keep on nursing the baby to prevent postpartum hemorrhage. She understood that. They left without saying thank you. I guess they were too frightened.

"The young woman was fortunate to have been taken to my aid station because I am sure there was no one within many miles who had the remotest idea how to deliver a baby presenting as a breech.

"The next morning, we got a report that the mother and baby were doing well and I received a couple of welcome bottles of Calvados from some of the locals.

"I probably will never know how they knew where my aid station was. The whole event got to be known, and it was written up in The Stars and Stripes. That was the only baby I delivered in my entire time in the Army."

When I returned to Normandy in 2003, fifty-nine years later, I thought it would be wonderful if I could find the "baby." I had not recorded the mother's name, since at the time, I did not think that I would survive. So what would have been the point? However, I did report the date and the event in a letter to my mother.

When the reporters interviewed me, they expressed considerable interest. In their articles, they mentioned my search. I had also written to the mayors of cities and towns in the area.

The articles produced an outpouring of interest that continues to today. There were letters of encouragement. There were letters from a number of women who thought they might be the one. Most of the letters were in French, so I had to get the help of a neighbor to translate. I answered every letter to get the maximum description of details remembered. Careful review found situations that did not agree with my recollections.

Francine's mother had a number of major wounds. I did not recall my patient having any wounds. Another woman said her mother remembered "sisters" helping her in a field hospital. I did not have a hospital. I merely had an aid station. There were no nurses or nuns in my aid station. So it went.

In December 2003 another article was written. It produced calls from Holland and England, but again I was disappointed. Good candidates had either different dates or circumstances.

The search goes on. I have had a chance to meet many wonderful people in my quest. The mayors and newspaper people have followed up with remarkable interest. I still have hopes of finding the "baby" now, some sixty years later.

Chapter 18

Ethics

All physicians are faced with making decisions; many of these are ethical in nature. As an obstetrician-gynecologist, I had my share of ethical dilemmas.

Early in my practice, before we had any means of prenatal diagnosis (like amniocentesis), I was confronted with a problem. A young mother who had a sad obstetrical history came to me as a patient. She was in her third pregnancy. Her first one ended in a spontaneous abortion. Her second ended in the birth of a severely compromised baby boy whose diagnosis was "gargoylism." I had not heard of it, but I learned that the baby appears fairly normal at birth, but rapidly develops coarse features, a large misshapen head, a curvature of the spine, a protuberant abdomen, a hernia of the umbilicus, an enlarged liver, clouding of the cornea, multiple cardiac abnormalities, dwarfism, and mental retardation. Now, this is more often called Hurler syndrome. The baby usually dies before the age of two. I learned that this syndrome is caused by a recessive gene, so both the mother and the father must have the gene for it to be expressed. It is rare for anyone to have this gene, and, of course, it would be exceedingly rare for two carriers of this gene to marry. The statistical expectation for these carriers is: one child with two normal chromosomes will be normal; two children will have one normal and one abnormal chromosome and therefore will be carriers without disease; and one child will have the disease.

Well, the woman under my care went close to term, and again delivered a baby with this horrible disease. It was essentially impossible for the patient to care for this terribly diseased child, even though she tried. The baby was placed in an institution recommended by her Catholic parish. The institution stated, in accepting this second child, that they could not afford to accept another, since the cost of caring for such a child was great. This was the most severely handicapped child I had ever seen or heard of.

About a year later, the young woman, in spite of using the rhythm system, returned to me, pregnant again. What to do? Most of her friends encouraged her to have an abortion, for two reasons: first, she would have to go through the stress of worrying through the pregnancy, and more important, she could have yet another gargoyle. She was persistent, being Catholic, and abortion in California was illegal, though I thought I might be able to manage to get permission in this case.

I said to her that, to the best of my knowledge, the odds described above pertained.

She decided to continue the pregnancy. Her priest agreed that she could have a sterilization after the pregnancy. The pregnancy seemed to go well, and I saw the patient often, mainly to reassure her. I noted that the baby was active in ways I usually associated with a healthy baby. Finally, labor started. Everyone who knew the situation followed labor and delivery anxiously. The baby was a normal male! Thank God.

* * *

Once, I delivered a baby with ninety percent of its brain absent. I made no effort to keep it alive, but did not have the will to kill it. Fortunately, it died in a short time after delivery.

* * *

We had a difficult time in my profession when abortion was illegal. I—and most of my colleagues—felt that a woman should have a right to choose whether she should be pregnant or not. The law in California permitted abortion if pregnancy endangered a mother's life. It is true that there are some conditions to which pregnancy is added to threaten a woman's life, but they are rare. Certain heart diseases come to mind. However, the main reason used before therapeutic abortion committees (which every hospital had) was that there was a threat of suicide, and this was verified by two psychiatrists. Actually, it is exceedingly rare that any woman commits suicide because of pregnancy. Psychiatrists, for the most part, were (like me) interested in protecting a woman's right to choose. So, they would write their letters to the therapeutic abortion committees that approved the procedure, and I, when the patient was mine, often did the operation. We were certainly not following the intent of the law, but we gynecologists had the approval of the committees, and could act with impunity. Eventually, the psychiatrists rebelled, but fortunately, at about that time, Roe vs. Wade passed.

* * *

When I was chief of staff at Mount Zion, it came to my attention that one of the members of our staff had repeatedly performed poorly in the care of his patients, sometimes by doing unjustified or poor surgery, and at other times by filing dishonest records. He had been warned in a formal way, but he persisted. He was a well-known doctor in the community, and he was respected for his religious work. Finally, I called a secret meeting of our most senior physicians, and stated that this man should not be permitted to work in our hospital, or I would quit as chief of staff and, if necessary, leave the staff. It was agreed that this doctor would no longer bring patients to our hospital, but we would bring no public action against him. This decision was presented to him by a man who had known him all his professional life, and who was a respected member of our staff. It was difficult to take such a strong action, because this man had brought a good number of patients to our hospital—but the move was necessary, so far as I was concerned.

* * *

Another well-known doctor I knew published a paper in a major medical journal. It was a well-written article, and I read it with interest. It was not on a subject that was current. Not long after it was published, I found that the same article—word for word—had been written ten years earlier by a distinguished physician in a much less-read journal. The doctor in question, who had copied the article and published it without giving credit to the author, applied for membership in an organization on the board of which I served. I refused to let him join. I did not want to discuss my reasons, but, in private, I explained my actions to the chairman. The application was turned down. All sorts of pressure was placed on me to change my vote. I was even threatened by a powerful banker. A group got me removed from the board. Interestingly, my replacement made an appointment with me to ask why I had been so adamant in my refusal. I swore him to secrecy and told him my reasons. He turned down the application. That applicant never made it into the organization. Occasionally, intentionally or unintentionally, authors include a phrase or even an idea without giving credit to the source, but a whole article is beyond any standard of decency.

* * *

A golfing friend brought his elderly mother to see me. She was eighty-two, and complained of a hugely distended abdomen. She was a small woman, and the large mass made getting around difficult. Various studies showed that the mass was a gigantic cyst. There was also some free fluid in the abdomen. Her internist said she was in reasonably good shape for a woman of her years. I told her that there was a reasonable chance that the tumor was benign, and that I could probably remove it, though that would demand a major operation. She asked me why I should do such an operation on an old woman.

I told her that eighty-two wasn't so old these days, and that she would be more comfortable with the tumor out. She asked to "think about it." Finally, she agreed to have the operation. She, of course, presented me with a problem: She was older, and would it be worth the risk of major surgery? I did the operation, and she lived actively to almost a hundred years.

* * *

In the practice of gynecology, I found that there were some difficult choices to be made in my office. Basically, the main concern of gynecologists is the health of the patient's pelvic organs. However, I have always felt that if saw a patient, I should be concerned for her general health as well. That concern demanded that a general examination, plus a pelvic examination, should be done—unless there was some reason not to. This attitude required that patients be completely undressed, and then be given a gown. Since the examination was intimate, it was traditionally advised that there be a female attendant in the room at the time of the examination. Such a precaution demanded that an office have at least two employees. In solo practice that becomes expensive, so I found that, with many patients, I felt confident that the examination could be done without an aid—as long as there was someone within shouting distance. That required intelligent selection of the patients. I never had a problem. Obviously, I always had an aid in the room with young women and new patients.

I felt strongly that there should be a minimum of exposure of the body of the patient. For example, I examined one breast at a time, keeping the other covered. In doing a pelvic examination, I kept as much of the anatomy as possible covered. Because examination of the pelvic organs requires careful examination of the external structures and introducing a finger or two into the vagina, it seemed vital to keep these examinations as gentle and as brief as possible. I never stayed in the room while a patient dressed or undressed.

* * *

Doctors have always, of necessity, been concerned with the economics of practice. In recent years, Medicare has set specific fees that a physician can charge for visits and procedures. If you have patients who do not have Medicare, you could not charge them more for the same items. That has led many physicians to perform minimal procedures, in order to enhance the income from a visit. For instance, a harmless skin tag could be removed and noted as a surgical biopsy, which would yield a significant fee. An endometrial biopsy could be called a dilatation, and curettage also giving a larger fee. I have always felt that such actions were not ethical, and they reflected poorly on the profession. Of course, our tissue committees have helped reduce much unnecessary surgery.

Probably, in all walks of life, there are times when one must make moral decisions. However, I think that in medicine those occasions come up more often, and we are frequently called upon to search our souls.

Chapter 19

Ace Bandages

During World War II, I was in command of a battalion aid station. We were called combat medics because we were part of the front lines. Our job was to pick up the wounded and get them out of danger as safely as possible. That usually involved controlling bleeding if possible, and giving the wounded man a cigarette if he was conscious, as well as a shot of morphine. The big problem was dealing with wounds that were often horrendous. The standard equipment for aid men included compressed bandages that expanded into a large square. They had been developed in World War I. These bandages had a strip of strong material at each corner, and the bandage would be held in place by tying the strips together. Within a day of treating the wounded, I found that such a bandage would not control bleeding well, and that it tended to slip, exposing the wound. Further, using adhesive tape was time-consuming and not efficient in controlling bleeding.

I had begun to think of this problem while we were in England preparing for the invasion of Normandy. I decided that I was probably going to go outside of regulations. I laid in a stock of elastic bandages, many more than were listed in our recommended supplies. When I got into action, I soon discovered that I was right. Elastic bandages would hold the old G.I. bandage firmly in place, and because of the pressure they exerted, they could help control blood loss. I had each of my aid men carry a knapsack loaded with these bandages. They also proved to be perfect in holding wounded extremities on splints. I had the men carry "wire ladder splints" that could be rolled up. These, with the aid of the Ace (elastic) bandage, saved many a limb—and often its function.

I was so impressed with the value of the elastic bandage that after the war, I always carried at least one with me when I was traveling, with extra in my luggage. There are always a couple in the first-aid sack in my car's trunk, and one in my golf bag.

Gwen and I were traveling on the Riviera in the '50s, and we were in our room in a small hotel. We heard a loud crash, followed by the sound of glass breaking. We thought there had been an automobile accident. Suddenly, we heard a loud voice just outside our door: "Au secours, au secours." I opened the door to see a large man lying on the floor with a huge gash in his thigh, from which blood was spurting. The man had walked through a large glass wall near our swimming pool. I put my hand over the spurting artery and asked Gwen to get a dressing and an Ace bandage from my supplies. I put on the dressing and held it firmly in place with the bandage. The bleeding was controlled. I splinted the leg and sent for an ambulance.

Soon a local doctor came. He wanted to place a tourniquet, but I would not let him, because I felt that if he cut off all circulation, the man might lose his leg. It was difficult to convince the French doctor, but I was adamant. The ambulance came, and the patient was taken to a local hospital. His son-in-law was a vascular surgeon. He flew down from Paris and repaired the severed artery. He gave me credit for possibly saving the man's life, but certainly for saving his leg. That evening, with the entire family of the wounded man at a large table in our dining room, I went over to ask how he was doing. All the women stood up, which I considered to be a major compliment in France. The hotel manager gave me a fine bottle of cognac, but the bandage was the real star.

Some time later, we had just returned from a trip to Mexico. I found that in our mail were a couple of letters intended for our neighbor. He lived across the street. Our front door opened on a steep hill, and it had been raining. I thought I would like to take our neighbor his mail. We had traveled a good deal that day, and I guess I was not functioning too well, for I slipped and fell in the wet street. I knew I had broken my leg. I stayed there, and a small boy came along. I asked him to call Gwen. Of course, she was alarmed. I told her to get a couple of Ace bandages and a long narrow cardboard box I had noted in our house. She carefully put my leg in the box and held it in place with the Ace bandages. I was transported to the emergency room of Mount Zion Hospital, where an X-ray showed the fracture, but it was in a perfect position, so that all that was needed was a more stable cast. Without the bandages, the bone might have moved out of position, which could have been dangerous. Again the lessons of the war helped.

We were in Argentina. Gwen was getting off a tour bus, and somehow tore back a large flap of skin on her arm. I had a small first-aid pack with me. I put some antibiotic cream on the arm, replaced the flap, applied a dressing that would not stick (Telfa), and held it in place with a small Ace bandage. The area, though quite large, healed well, and there was no scar.

Our golf course had recently been remodeled. The sand traps had been made much deeper, especially those near the greens. This made the approaches to the traps steep. When there was rain, the steep slopes became slippery, and were dangerous. One day, one of the members of my foursome slipped into a sand trap, and we all knew he had broken his leg just above the ankle. I fashioned a splint from a golf umbrella I had, and held the leg in a good position with an Ace bandage. An ambulance came and picked up the man. His fracture healed in reasonable time, and he was back of the golf course in about six weeks.

So, I guess I got something out of World War II beside my hatred of war. Battlefield experience helped me solve problems in the peacetime world.

Chapter 20

Sex

Early on in my medical career, my major concerns were associated with obstetrics and its problems. Then I had a steadily increasing interest in cancer. However, almost daily I was confronted with sexual problems.

Patients are reluctant to discuss their sexual concerns with doctors; however, people in my speciality develop rapport with their patients, especially after the long relationship that develops in the course of a pregnancy. Women were often fearful of hurting the baby with intercourse during pregnancy. I was confident that it most cases sexual intercourse was safe, but I often had to instruct patients to try positions other than the common "missionary" position. The patients welcomed my reassurance, and often told me that I had broken up some of the marital tension that can develop in the course of a pregnancy. After delivery, there was often a problem related to the stitches that repair the vagina. Again, instructions in how to have minimal distress at that time was again welcomed. Sexual satisfaction can be achieved in other ways than vaginal intercourse. I found that "giving permission" to experiment often produced remarkable effects.

I had one patient who on two occasions had severe abdominal pain after otherwise satisfactory sexual relations. When I saw her, it was important to be sure first that she was not pregnant, because she could have her symptoms from a ruptured tubal pregnancy. From her history and lab test, there was no likelihood of pregnancy. The most rapid diagnostic test I could do was to insert a needle through the vagina into her abdomen to evaluate the abdominal contents. I recovered blood, which did not clot. If the blood had clotted, it could have been from inserting the needle. But the fact that the blood did not clot meant that it had mixed with peritoneal fluid. So the diagnosis was that a cyst of the ovary had been ruptured during intercourse. I checked her blood count immediately and regularly. She was not anemic, nor did she have a significant drop in her hemoglobin. Naturally, she became very anxious about intercourse. I told her to abandon the missionary position, and to try intercourse on her side, or with her superior. From then on, she had no trouble, and enjoyed sex without fear. She remains a grateful patient.

Early in my practice, the major available contraceptives were the vaginal diaphragm and condoms, or various forms of the rhythm method.

Not long into my practice, oral contraceptives were introduced. This form of contraception started an era of sexual freedom. A complication of increased sexual freedom was an increase in vaginal infections. However, we were rapidly developing ways to overcome the usual vaginal infections when they were recognized.

I had a few sexual professionals as patients. The first was an attractive young woman who supported herself and her young daughter by being a "call girl," mostly for the St. Francis Hotel and Hilton Hotel clients. She had a deal with bellmen in those hotels. She knew all there was to know about contraception and infections. Her main fear was of physical harm. Her fears were never realized. She was a good judge of character.

The whole scene changed with the introduction of HIV/AIDS. Having partners use condoms became extremely important. This was often difficult. I told women, professional and non, that if they were not absolutely sure about their partner, they must have the men use condoms, and to report to their doctor if the condom failed in any way.

I recall one patient who was in her late thirties, and who described herself as "easy," by which she meant that she could reach a sexual climax with ease. Her problem was in finding a partner. She was attractive, but fairly tall. So now I wanted to be able to find the best way for her and women like her to find suitable male companions. I became an expert in knowing about church groups and groups who are interested in the theater, rock-climbing, or a whole array of social activities.

But the most frequent problem in my practice was the complaint of women not being able to reach orgasm. When a patient presented me with that problem, I often asked her to stay around until I had time to talk with her. I never discussed anything sexual in an examining room, but waited until I had a desk between me and the patient. I found that instructions for partners often helped. But I think where my advice was most successful was in encouraging patients to try experimenting, and to do anything that felt good. If I could get these women away from their inhibitions, amazing things often happened. This was especially true for my older patients, who often complained that their male partners were frustrated by no longer being able to have an erection, even with Viagra or similar drugs. I received thank you notes and presents from couples for whom manual or oral stimulation produced wondrous results.

For a practicing gynecologist, it turns out that, so far as a patient is concerned, helping her to solve her sexual problems seems as important as protecting her from cancer.

Chapter 21

French Legion of Honor

The publication of the 35th Infantry Division in which I served, the Santa Fe Express "35th Divisionnaire," comes to me regularly. Some time in 2005, there was a notice that combat veterans of World War II would be eligible for The French Legion of Honor. If one was interested, he should send some basic information to the local French Consulate for consideration. I sent my information in. It was acknowledged, but nothing happened. Obviously, there was no guarantee that there would be a medal awarded.

In the late afternoon of Friday, October 26, 2007, I got a phone call from the French Consulate in San Francisco. The man asked if it would be possible for me to come by the consulate that afternoon or evening. The new consul general would like to speak with me. He would be leaving for Paris that evening. If it were not possible, they would try to arrange something the following week; however, it was clearly implied that the visit on the 26th would be desirable. I said that I lived close by the Consulate, and would it be convenient if I were to come right over? The distance was only six or seven blocks from where I live. He was pleased with that. I put on a decent blazer and took off.

The Consulate is on the fourth floor of a nice building on Bush Street. I rang the bell, and was greeted by a young man immediately. There was a reception area, from which I was taken to a large area with a number of desks. I was introduced to various members of the staff. I was surprised to see this many workers there this late in the day. Finally, Deputy Consul General Patrice Servantie introduced me to the new consul general, Pierre-François Mourier. He met me graciously, and took me and Patrice into his office—a fairly large space, with elegant leather furnishing. I was shows to a sofa facing a large desk, behind which sat

Pierre. He is a medium-sized, well-dressed man who speaks good English with a pleasant French accent.

After some brief small talk, Pierre asked if it would be possible for me to come to Washington D.C. during the week of December 5th. I said I thought it would be possible. He then said that the new president of France, Nicolas Sarkozy, was to be in Washington briefly, and he would like to award me the French Legion of Honor. That was a mind-blowing surprise. After I pulled myself together, I said that this was very short notice to get air reservations. He said that would be no problem. They would take care of that. Then I said that I could not go to such an important occasion without my wife. He said they would gladly provide for her. I mentioned the fact that hotel reservations might be difficult. He said that they would take care of that. He also stated that they would get us to the airport, and see that we got to the hotel in DC. It all sounded wonderful.

There was the some brief talk about the event. Essentially, there were to be seven veterans of World War II chosen from around the country. I was to represent the Western United States. He said that they were particularly impressed with the fact that someone with my background—being a student and in training as an ob/gyn intern—could adapt to combat conditions, and to be recognized for doing an excellent job. I asked how I should dress for the occasion. I said I could still fit into my uniform, if they would like that. He thought the uniform would be excellent for the presentation of the medal, but on the following day we were to go to congress to hear Mr. Sarkozy speak ,and that would be followed by a luncheon. For those two events, I was to wear the medal on a business suit.

I floated home. Naturally, Gwen and I were excited. We quickly notified our children. The next day, my daughter, Jan, began making plans to join us. I checked with the consulate, and they said they would be able to reserve a room for her in our hotel—and they also could get her on the same plane. They also said that we would have to pay for her, which were happy to do.

My son Jim and his wife live in Chico. On hearing the news, they immediately made plans to join us. They made their own reservations, since they have a relationship with Hyatt. My son John was out of town at a medical meeting, but when he returned, he decided to join us. By this time, though, he had great difficulty getting a plane reservation, but he finally got on a "red eye" arriving late at night on the 4th of November. He could not find a hotel room, but the people at the hotel where we were staying suggested he share a room with our daughter. They could put in a rollaway.

We were to leave on the morning of the 5th of November. On that morning, we were packed with carry-on luggage; Jan, who lives only a short distance away, joined us. Pierre appeared on time, with a French government van and driver. Pierre would be traveling with us. We were traveling on United Airlines. Gwen and I are Frequent Fliers. We had checked on our seats and found that we were sitting behind each other. I called repeatedly to get the seats improved. Finally, I got a supervisor, who said she would put in a request. Jan had an aisle seat in the middle of economy class. Pierre had a terrible seat far back in economy. (The French instructions to consulates is that they must travel economy. I later told Pierre that he should get an agent who could get him much better economy seats in the future.) At the gate, just before boarding, Gwen and I were paged, and we were presented with seats far back in business class, which was wonderful for us. The trip was uneventful. At arrival in DC, Pierre located the man who was to meet us, using his cell phone. The man had been at the luggage collecting point, but we, of course, had carry-on. The man, a French major, drove us to our hotel, the Park Hyatt. Though the woman at reception gave us a lot of trouble, mainly because of her inexperience, we were taken to our rooms. Gwen and I had a pleasant, small suite. Much to our joy, Jan had a double room with two beds, which would work well when my son arrived much later.

Gwen and I went to the bar for a snack. While sitting there, a gentleman came over and asked if we were there for the medal, and we said we were. He introduced himself as another recipient. He is an American Indian, and he was traveling with his chief and former chief. His name is Charles Shay. He is a remarkable man. He was in the first wave in the invasion of North Africa, in the first wave in the invasion of Sicily, and in the first wave in the invasion of Normandy. All of his wartime service was with the 1st Infantry Division. Later on, he served in The Korean War. He was modest about all of this. It was a good introduction to the type of people who were to get the medal on the next day.

We decided to spend the next morning doing nothing special. The big event was to occur in the afternoon of the 5th of November. At breakfast, and in the various areas, we had a chance to meet the other recipients. Senator Inouye was the only one not staying at our hotel, since he has his own residence in DC. James Hill was with the 29th Division, which was in the first wave at Omaha Beach. Henry Langrehr was a parachutist who landed behind the German lines with the 82nd Airborne the day before D-Day. He was wounded captured, hospitalized, put to work in a coal mine, escaped with a buddy who was killed. He was wounded two more times. George Thompson had a remarkable record as a mortar man; a small man from New York, he had memorized the eye chart in order to get in the service. He was wounded, captured, exchanged, and returned to fight on. These were the sort of people who made me feel doubly honored to be included.

We were to be at the residence of the French ambassador at 3:30 p.m. Naturally, we were to leave in plenty of time. A small fleet of vans came to pick us up. Jan and John traveled with Gwen and me. Jim and Sheryl were to meet us at the residence. By chance, we all arrived at the same time.

The residence is a splendid building built in 1905, and bought by France in 1936. It sits on five acres of lush gardens. We all went through security quickly. They were well-prepared. There were gracious people everywhere, who introduced themselves and took us to a large room, where the presentation was to take place. The medal recipients were seated in the first row of chairs. The seats had been previously assigned. Other chairs were placed for family and close friends. The large space gradually filled with men in uniforms of France and the United States. There were more photographers than I have ever seen in such a relatively small area. While we were waiting for President Sarkozy to arrive, two of us were interviewed at length. I was one. Jim and Sheryl came to watch.

President Sarkozy was only in Washington for 26 hours; he had an extremely busy schedule, so it was not surprising that he was late by twenty minutes or so. He came in a relaxed manner. He was introduced by a French officer. He spoke in French, even though he speaks good English. He had an excellent translator, who timed her translations perfectly. Essentially, he expressed the gratitude of France for what we and the people with whom we fought did for France in saving it from the Germans. He then gave a brief biography of each of the recipients. He showed a sense of humor when he said that Charles Shay, the American Indian, had a ancestor in the seventeenth century who was a French trapper, which gave him deeper roots to France than Sarkozy had.

He then went down the line of us. He would pin a medal on our lapel, kiss us on each cheek, and give us an embrace. When he did that with me, I said "*Merci.*" He quickly responded, "Thank you, John, you are a hero." I was impressed that he had learned my name.

He then had his picture taken with all of us and quietly left. There then was a splendid reception, centered in the dining room. It had beautiful, pale-green boiserie. The food and drink were sumptuous. There was real foie gras and elegant French champagne, plus all kinds of other tidbits and wine. I was pleased to see that my children made themselves at home and talked with various guests, especially the French, many of whom were veterans of World War II. I had the opportunity to talk with the commanding general of the 10th Mountain Division, in which I served before being transferred to the 35th for the invasion of Normandy. The general looked like a college student to me, but his division is one of the most respected. I told him that what I had learned in the 10th Mountain had helped me and those I cared for survive in the Ardennes in the Battle of the Bulge. We left on schedule.

Gwen and I had arranged dinner that evening at a restaurant where we had celebrated our fiftieth wedding anniversary in 1996. We all arrived at the same time. After a bit of negotiation, we ended up in the same area where we had celebrated our big anniversary. Obviously, there was much to discuss. All were excited. On the following day, Gwen and I were invited to hear the French president address the US Congress. Tickets were limited. Sheryl had been working to get tickets for her, Jim, John, and Jan. We didn't think she would be able to do it.

On the following morning, Gwen and I were picked up. We hoped to see our children later, or maybe in San Francisco. All of the medal honorees were wearing their medals as instructed. We were taken to an elegant reception room in the Capitol building. Much to our pleasant surprise, we saw Sheryl, Jim, John, and Jan as we marched past. Somehow or other, Sheryl had obtained tickets for all of them, even though the gallery was sold out. In the reception room, Nancy Pelosi came by to congratulate all of us, and to have her picture taken with the group, but before she did that, she greeted Gwen and me—her constituents—and had her picture taken with us. We then went to take our seats in the diplomatic gallery. Gwen and I were assigned to the first row, much to our surprise and joy. All of our children were seated right behind us. Medal winners were supposed to get one seat, but somehow Sheryl had swung the deal.

The congressional room and balcony were filled. Both houses of Congress and the Supreme Court members were there. The diplomatic areas were full. President Sarkozy was introduced by Nancy Pelosi, who was chair.

He spoke beautifully in French. We all had earphones with instant translation. He got repeated applause, and often standing ovations. It had been a long time since a French president had come to the United States, and it had been a long time since there had been something to cheer about. He stressed the French debt to the United States, particularly in World War II. He also made a major point of how we should work together to improve the environment and world peace.

After the congressional session, the medal winners and one guest were invited to a special luncheon at the French embassy. The embassy is a working building—interesting, but quite modern. We were all seated at assigned seats. Present in addition to the medal winners and their guest were French veterans, some military men, and various members of the diplomatic staff.

The luncheon was pleasant. One of the French guests, an older man, told Gwen that he enjoyed meeting and talking with Jan on the previous day.

At the end of the meal, I thought that I should say something, especially because President Sarkozy had called me the "dean" of the group. I made a short speech of thanks for the gracious way we had been treated.

It was then time to catch our plane home. To our horror, we had heard that Jan and John's luggage had been put with ours by mistake. Somehow the error was picked up, and the security chief from our hotel picked up their luggage, picked them up, and drove them to the airport, which was wonderful for them. We went with Pierre. We all met at the airport, where we learned about the good news with John and Jan.

We arrived home tired but still excited. We were met at the San Francisco airport. The driver took Gwen and me home, then Jan, then Pierre. We did not sleep too well. Our minds were busy reliving those splendid days.

Word got around the medical center and elsewhere, and I began to get congratulatory letters and phone calls, but there was no significant newspaper mention of Sarkozy's visit.

In early December, I got a call from John Koopman, a reporter for the San Francisco Chronicle. He wanted to interview me. We set a date, and he came to our apartment. He is a big, pleasant man and a former Marine, though I think that once a Marine, always a Marine. We had a pleasant, long session. He had been embedded with the 1st Marine Division in the invasion of Iraq. These things being so, he seemed to understand what it is that a combat medic does. He asked if he could send a photographer. Of course, I had no objection. She came a couple of days later, and must have taken a hundred shots. In a few days, John called to say that his editor liked the story. So, I thought there would be a piece about me in some Sunday supplement. On the 17th of December, early in the morning, I got a call from my son John and his wife Louise, who said that I was on the front page of the San Francisco Chronicle, including a picture. There it was, with a long article that could not have been more complimentary.

Now the phone calls and mail really poured in. Various people at the medical center, Doctor Bishop, the chancellor, Senator Feinstein, the consul general of Belgium, who presented me with a signed picture of her king and queen, and so many more. The San Francisco Gynecological Society asked to honor me. The Internet contained much more, including many pictures.

At this point in my life, I was not prepared for such attention, but it has been wonderful.

Chapter 22

Cancer

My interest in cancer began when I was in training. My professor, Doctor Traut, involved me in the development of the vaginal smear as a way of diagnosing cervical and uterine cancer, and probably more important, as a way to find precancerous lesions. Also, from my earliest times in the Department of Obstetrics and Gynecology, I found that we were a center for dealing with cancer of the genital organs. The largest number of our cancers were cervical (at the mouth of the uterus). When I started, our means of treatment included various forms of irradiation, usually a combination of radium and X-ray. The other modality was surgery. The radical hysterectomy known as a Wertheim was used. It required great skill and knowledge. When I first began to be involved with these cancers, we did not have blood banks, and there were no antibiotics. We were just beginning to use sulfa drugs against infection. Penicillin use started after the war. We tried to find donors of the same blood type as our patient. The house staff, usually an intern, would crossmatch the patient's blood with that of the potential donor. We were just beginning to learn about the Rh system and other subgroups, so at times, there were major unexpected reactions. In spite of these difficulties, our department had a remarkable series of surgeries, with results very close to those now obtained with sophisticated blood banks and a wide variety of antibiotics. We had to be very careful in deciding which patients would be good candidates for surgery, because complications were significant and often life-endangering. The first paper I ever wrote was at the end of my residency, and it was a review of every patient ever treated with irradiation at UCSF. Because our senior residents learned to do the radical operation for cervical cancer, we learned to be unusually good surgeons. We could apply those skills.

At that time, X-ray therapy was crude. There were severe skin reactions, and often there was damage to non-cancerous body structures. Gradually the machines became more sophisticated, and could target the problem areas more precisely, but that took many years.

But a major change was on the way, due to the acceptance of The Papanicolau-Traut smears. Early in my training, Doctor Traut showed me smears with cells that he felt were cancer cells mixed with normal cells. I was assigned the task of finding where the abnormal cells came from. This often required multiple biopsies, and then looking at them through a microscope to find cells that matched those in the smear. This proved that the unusual cells in the smear were from cancerous or precancerous areas. My original slides still exist in the collection of Doctor Karen Smith-McCune.

The next project given me was to make slides that could be projected to show these findings. Such slides had never been made. I worked long hours with a technician who was trying to make projection slides of blood smears. We were finally able to make good slides. These were the first ever done for this purpose.

It became necessary to get the word out that smears could lead to early diagnosis of cervical and uterine cancer, and even of precursors. Early in my practice, when Doctor Traut thought I could spare the time, he arranged for the American Cancer Society to send me around the state to talk up the smears. It was not easy. The pathologists all said they needed tissue. Doctor Traut began to talk at national meetings. Finally, starting with our chief of pathology at UC, the smears were accepted. With that, cervical cancer and its precursors were discovered early, and as a result invasive cervical cancer has become extremely rare in the United States. We rarely have to do the radical operation or use irradiation for that disease. What a blessing!

I continued to have an interest in cancer and cancer therapy when I went into practice. One of my first patients was the wife of an owner of a well-known bar. She came to my office with an invasive cancer of the uterine cervix. I consulted with Doctor Traut. He advised external irradiation, followed by a radical operation. So, one of the first operations I ever did in private practice was the most difficult procedure being done in my specialty. My bill for the operation was large for the time, $500. The operation went perfectly. On her first postoperative visit, she came to my office and paid her bill in cash. That was the most cash that I had seen since the war. She did well. Her only problem was that she developed trouble with one hip related to the irradiation, so she used a cane. The first major paper I ever wrote was on complications of irradiation. I reviewed every patient with cancer of the cervix who had been treated with irradiation at UCSF. For this patient, although she had a hip problem, her cancer did not recur. I followed her for many years, and she sent Christmas gifts each year until she died of heart disease.

When I became chief of staff at Mount Zion Medical Center in 1975, I felt that the institution should be involved in basic research. Until then, the major research had been in clinical cardiology. I thought that we should start a program that would have as a major goal cancer research. It was obvious that there was no one at Mount Zion who could tell me the route research was taking, so I went to Doctor Bishop at UCSF. Mike Bishop was highly respected, and he, with his colleague Harold Varmus, were interested in cancer genes. He had not yet been awarded the Nobel Prize. He made clear to me that the future in cancer research and in biological research lay in the understanding and use of molecular biology. He encouraged me to search for someone with knowledge in that area. He also felt that to lead such a program I should find an MD. The search was started immediately. We finally selected a brilliant young endocrinologist, Ira Goldfine. Though his primary interest had been in diabetes, in our discussions, he agreed with the premise that future breakthroughs in our understanding of cancer were to be found in molecular biology. He agreed to work in that direction, while not relinquishing his interest in diabetes.

We built a laboratory for Ira in the lower portion of a building that had had a clinic on the first floor and a cardiac research center on the second, The Brunn Institute. Doctor Brunn was a pioneering chest surgeon. The first major piece of equipment for the new lab was an electron microscope. Such instruments were rare then, and expensive. I was able to purchase it from my fund. Gradually, we added high speed centrifuges and facilities for cell cultures, which were just beginning to be possible in quantity. We were able to generate a talented staff with grants and the help of my fund.

As progress was made, it became obvious that there would be a great value in expanding our research; however, that would require more space. I was able to hire a firm of experienced architects to design a building on an available site at Mount Zion. It had to be several stories tall, because the space available was limited. I was promised major funding with help from a new friend, Julian Levi. Julian had been a major player at the University of Chicago Law School, and he knew many influential people. He had come to San Francisco to join the Hastings Law School faculty. He had become a friend of my parents, and so I got to know and respect him. When I went to the board of directors of Mount Zion with my plan, they stated that they did not want money spent on a research building when the hospital was in poor economic shape. They asked a potential supporter of my plan to join the board of directors. He later told me that he was not about to put money into Mount Zion, which he felt was failing, in part because of poor management. My building was not built.

Not long after that, Mount Zion joined with The University of California Medical Center. This proved to be a necessary route for Mount Zion, since there was a shortage of money. The next step was to see how the merger could work most efficiently. The university wanted the intensive care nursery, which I had started. It was a source of considerable income, and its staff was superior to what was available at UC at the time. If they took the nursery, I did not think we should have obstetrics at Mount Zion. It was obvious that any obstetrical service in a major city must have a superior nursery to survive.

At this point, being asked to give up obstetrics and the newborn nursery, I asked that the cancer program be moved to Mount Zion. Cancer research and treatment had not been areas of special interest at UC, with research being the weakest.

Almost immediately, it was decided to build a large cancer research building across the street from Mount Zion. Perhaps more important was the search for a leader of the cancer program. That position was filled by Frank McCormick, a brilliant choice.

The splendid building was completed in surprisingly quick fashion. Doctor McCormick assembled a remarkable group of researchers, including the best available at UC, particularly Joe Gray, supplemented by a group from Great Britain, including Gerard Evan and Alan Balmain. The process was accelerated by the support of donors who provided funds for endowed chairs with the title of "distinguished professor." Such chairs require the donation of $2.5 million. (Recently, The Kerner Cancer Fund was able to provide the funds for such a chair, held now by John Chan, who has led the women's cancer program at UCSF to be among the best in our country.)

The need for a center for the care of cancer patients was met by converting an old hospital, Maimonides, which is next door to the research building. Margaret Tempero, a brilliant clinician, was recruited to lead the clinical program, and a new building was planned for the clinical care of patients. A cancer center was now possible. It soon became one of twelve to gain the coveted recognition as an NCI-designated cancer center.

In 2002, a remarkable series of events occurred. The research group I had been sponsoring had noted that the more severe breast cancers had a higher number of receptors for insulin. This stimulated an increased interest in breast cancer.

An organization that recognized our interest in cancer sent us a group of compounds to be studied as possible anti-cancer drugs. Two of those agents seemed to be effective against cancer in cell cultures. One of them had been tried as a treatment for diabetes, but proved to be no better than other agents. However, while it was being tried, it was found that it could be tolerated by humans in significant doses. This drug we called NDGA because of its chemical structure. We found that it showed great promise as a treatment for prostate, breast, and pancreatic cancers. It is a natural product found in the creosote bush of the Southwest. We found that NDGA kills cancer cells by inhibiting cancer proteins called RTKs. RTKs sit on the surface of cancer cells, and when switched on, cause cancer cells to grow rapidly and spread throughout the body. The major action of NDGA is to switch off these RTKs, causing cancer cell death.

We soon found that we had a good deal of preliminary work to do before we could begin clinical testing of the drug. We had to synthesize the NDGA so that we could better understand how it worked. Later it might be modified to be even more effective. We had to develop a plan to obtain the drug in the quantity necessary for clinical trials. It was necessary to learn how to create a Phase I trial group to ensure that

NDGA would not cause major side effects in cancer patients. We had to plan to get a patent. We needed to obtain the support of the legal team at UCSF. We had to structure an agreement with the university as to how to divide any future profits from the sale of the drug, should there be any.

While this was proceeding, I asked the personnel working with me to address the problem of evaluating the effects of our medicine. Being impatient, I hoped to be able to evaluate our drug's efficacy without having to wait many months or even years. The staff came up with two solutions: First, if we started even preliminary studies on patients with prostate cancer, we could measure effectiveness by a fall in PSA, which is a good indicator for activity with that cancer. If there were a decrease, we could be confident that the drug was working. Second, an ingenious worker discovered that he could get our target receptors in breast cancer cells to "light up" when stained properly. So if an initial breast biopsy was positive for cancer, and if the patient was then given NDGA, a second, more extensive biopsy, could be stained to find if we were hitting the target.

We planned to start trials as soon as possible, first using prostate patients with cancer, in whom therapy had failed. While we were seeing if there were any serious side effects of the drug (Phase I), after a month we could check to see if the PSA decreased.

Now, we had to demonstrate to the UCSF urologists that NDGA was a potentially effective agent against prostate cancer, and to persuade them to participate in Phase 1 clinical trials. Once convinced, they agreed to provide a study group of patients for whom other treatment had failed. Equally important, they agreed to provide a well-qualified nurse-supervisor, and to do most of the requisite laboratory work. We hired an expert to write up the protocol for us to proceed with our trials. This was modified by the urologists to fit their patient population. We were set to go, or so I thought.

The senior urologists, whom I considered to be the best in our country, were aboard. The head of the cancer center approved of what we were doing as did the cancer center's Committee for Human Research. The FDA gave us approval to proceed with clinical trials. All we needed now was the approval of the university's Human Research Board (RIB). They turned us down. We were dumbfounded. The basis of the rejection was presented by a consultant, not the whole committee. Our point man in the process answered all questions as requested. They turned us down again. They questioned why we would try our drug on people who might be treated in some other way. We tried to explain that these patients had failed all previous treatment, and had been selected by the urology people who specialized in cancer. *They turned us down a third time.* I could not believe the arrogance of turning down the best group of urologists in the country, not to mention my team, who had done the basic work. I enlisted the help of the chief of the cancer center and the chief of Urology, and I approached the chancellor through his assistant. These delays had held us up for three months. We planned to send a delegation to meet with the committee, which, up to this point, accepted only material in writing. Our frustration continued to grow. We had an agent that we had good reason to feel would be effective against a number of cancers. Our drug stood to bring credit upon our university, as well as financial gain. It was the first anti-cancer agent developed at UC. A huge amount of work had been done in getting to this point. Plans for getting the medication to the patients had been completed, and financial support had been worked out. This committee had driven us to distraction, as it had others in the past.

The committee agreed to a plan I suggested. On December 11, 2003, our biggest gun, Eric Small, and the point man in this anti-cancer effort, Brian Rim, met with the RIB (Human Research Board) committee. Eric was a professor of medicine and urology, and is considered one of the most respected doctors in the field of prostate cancer in the United States. Brian was an assistant professor, and already a rising star. They felt that they answered the questions that had arisen, and that they had a good sense from the committee about changes that had to be made to address their concerns. They believed that they could achieve their goals in a week, after which we could move ahead. I still could not get over the fact that members of this committee questioned the judgment of Eric Small. He would be the first person the men would consult if they had prostate cancer. Of course, one of the members was a woman who wanted the patients to be treated with radiation, even though Eric did not think it was indicated at this time. It almost looked as if she wanted more business for her department, rather than the health and welfare of the patients.

After wasting almost three months, the committee agreed to our proceeding. We were relieved, but we regretted the time and energy that were expended unnecessarily. We rapidly completed the paperwork necessary, so that we could negotiate the production of pills containing NDGA. We decided that a gel cap would be least likely to be associated with gastric irritation. The company that had the supply of NDGA was only too willing to cooperate in our desire to proceed rapidly with our trials.

We continued to press for trials on men with advanced prostate cancer first. Having heard of our success to this point, we got much increased interest from the breast cancer group. Actually, in our preclinical trials the agent looked most promising for breast cancer; however, we decided to try the drug's efficacy against prostate cancer first, because the PSA test would be an early indicator of success or failure, and because the prostate cancer group was so well-organized and supported.

I could hardly wait to get started. But we were still delayed. The material had to be put into capsules. The company we had selected to do the work had a backlog. After some of the capsules were made, they had to be tested to be sure that they would dissolve properly, in order to deliver the drug. It was estimated that this whole process would take until June 1, three months away. I tried, but could find no way to accelerate the process.

Meanwhile, because of a recent infusion of money from Mary Jane Briton, we could begin plans for testing NDGA on breast cancer patients. We could also proceed with studies on our second anti-cancer agent, which was showing great promise in the laboratory.

I remained restless, and anxious to get moving on treating patients. I became increasingly aware of the urgency, since a number of friends and acquaintances were suffering with advanced cancer. They all feared the terrible reactions to conventional therapy with drugs and irradiation, which, so far, had not provided many cures that could not otherwise be achieved by radical surgery.

On Friday, March 12, 2004, Ira Goldfine and I met with Hope Rug, a remarkably well-trained oncologist with a special interest in breast cancer. She was aware of the work we had been doing with NDGA, and was enthusiastic in working with us to devise a program whereby we could do trials with our drug in breast cancer patients. We agreed that we should decide on a combination of two drugs. I had been convinced before the meeting that the ultimate goal of achieving cancer cure would most certainly require two drugs, or possibly three. Probably the best combination would be of our drug, combined with one that interfered with blood supply to the tumor (antiangiogenesis).

There was an exciting future. We hoped to be on the cutting edge of an entirely new approach in the battle against cancer. Chuck Ryan took over the role of leader in the prostate group. He was the most enthusiastic clinician we had met.

In June 2004, we got samples of pills containing the proper amount of NDGA. We selected the smallest of the three types offered. We now needed the production of a quantity that would get our Phase 1 trials started. We also had to get the FDA approval for these pills. We did not feel that the FDA would be a problem at this point. I was anxious, of course, to get going. We had lost another month in waiting for the production of the pills. We hoped that patients would begin receiving the pills during the month of July. That was not to be. The various tests and procedures necessary required that we had to postpone administration of our drug once again. The trials were set to begin in October 2004.

In the meantime, pediatric neurologists have found that NDGA has proven to be effective against neuroblastoma, a dreaded solid tumor of nerve tissues in children. It is often far advanced when discovered, and there is no known cure. It can occur almost anywhere in the body. They hope to start using it in trials as soon as Phase 1 trials are completed. Drugs to be used in children usually must be tried first in adults.

We had suggested to the nasopharyngeal tumor group at UC that they join us in our trials. They proved not to be interested. Recently, we heard that a variation of NDGA has been effective in reducing nasopharyngeal tumors by cancer researchers in India.

We thought all barriers had been cleared. Our first thirty patients suffer from prostate cancer that has not responded to any accepted therapy. There was now a growing group of cancer experts who believed that we had therapeutic agents of great promise. I prayed that that was true.

After yet another month, the FDA approved the pills. We then ordered a supply from Insmed for the first thirty patients. It took them about a month to produce and send the pills to our pharmacy.

We were now into January. In the meantime, Doctor Ryan had been notified by the Department of Defense (DOD) that he was to receive a grant of $700,000 for which he had applied. He began to receive half his salary from that grant in October 2004. Just when we were ready to start our trials, Ryan received word from the DOD that they wanted to review our protocols. We were surprised to hear that. We thought that if they had any reservations, they would have made them known before they began sending money. We received word that the reviewer would begin the review in about two weeks. After three weeks, the reviewer stated that she had started the review on a Saturday, and that we would hear from her in the next week. We did not hear for two weeks, when she asked for some additional information. The frustration continued to mount. We were now into the month of April 2005—almost a year after we had thought we could start our tests on people.

At this point the National Institutes of Health (NIH) informed us that they would like to fund the project. We knew that we could not accept funding from two sources. We also felt that the NIH was more prestigious than the DOD. After extensive consultations with all seniors involved, we found that there was universal agreement to send back what money we had received from the DOD, accept the grant from the NIH, and get going, which we planned to do. It was now May 2005. We were ready to start administering NDGA to men with advanced prostate cancer. Everyone involved was told to get moving.

Eric Small was the leader for the prostate cancer project. After various trials, Doctor Small made an excellent choice for the manager of the project—Charles ("Chuck") J. Ryan, MD. Doctor Ryan moved rapidly to organize the test group.

New drugs go through three phases of evaluation. The first phase is to search for toxicity. Because we were dealing with men with advanced prostate cancer, we could get some idea as to whether our drug was effective by seeing if the PSA would change. PSA measures an antigen which rises in the presence of prostate cancer. It is not a perfect measure, but it certainly gives a suggestion as to the direction the cancer is going.

The plan for testing the drug for toxicity follows: The test group was divided into subgroups of three. Our calculated goal was to eventually reach a level of 2 grams a day of NDGA. The first patient was given a dose of .75 grams daily for twenty-eight days. When he had no reaction, a second man was added, and he too had no reaction. A third followed, with the same result. A second group followed, with an increased dose of 1.25 grams daily. They had the same results. So far there was no significant change in PSAs, nor was any expected. A third group was then given a dose of 1.75 grams per day. Even though this was not our calculated dose, the first man in this group had his PSA reduced in half by the end of twenty-eight days. Then the second man in this group had a similar reduction. Everyone involved in the project was excited. This was the first time that men who had failed all other treatment had a reduction in PSA. This was even before we had reached our calculated therapeutic dose. The third man in the group did not have a significant change. However, two out of three at this level was impressive.

More pills were ordered, and the next group is to receive 2.25 mg per day. The men already tested will be given the option to continue at their level until Phase 1 is completed, when they might increase their dose.

Because of the success of the evaluation to date, the pediatricians are moving ahead with a program to use NDGA on children with neuroblastoma, a tumor for which no cure is available to date. Also, the breast cancer group is preparing to test the drug, particularly on patients who are resistant to Tamoxifen. There has been much excitement in the cancer center.

Our efforts in developing this drug have proved valuable in another way. We have perfected a pathway for getting medicines from the laboratory to the patient. In so doing, we have enhanced the funding abilities of the cancer center at UCSF, who can show that they are engaging in the vital use of our knowledge of cancer molecular biology to provide new therapies for cancer. It is wonderful for me to have been part of this progress after sixty years of interest.

Phase 1 was completed, and showed no serious effects from NDGA, and there was evidence that there was significant improvement in PSA levels. One man who had been taking the drug in the trials had lowered his PSA significantly. He stopped the drug because he did not get more pills, and his PSA rose to very high levels. We obtained permission to start on Phase 2. Because it was going well, we began to consider Phase 3, which requires a large group of patients, and which is very expensive, estimated to be at least $20 million. To this point, I had been able to fund a major portion of the costs from The Kerner Cancer Fund. However, there was no way I could fund a Phase 3. I consulted with Frank McCormick, the chief of cancer at UCSF, and with others. They advised me to form a company. I said, "You expect me to form a company at ninety years of age?" The reply was, "Yes John."

I was told that the first thing I should do is to find a CEO. The choice of my small group was Tom White. Tom had been CEO of a successful company like ours was to be. He agreed. A plan of development was set in place.

We hired a top-flight law firm—Wilson Sonsini Goodrich & Rosati—and our articles of incorporation were written by Michael O'Donnell, a member of the firm who was known to Tom. Tom then collected a group of top-flight people to join the firm, and to be consultants. These included the chief of cancer at UCSF, Frank McCormick. To my surprise, none of these people asked for payment in advance, or even when they had performed valuable services. They all said they would be paid when we were funded. That showed great confidence in our company.

Our original board was just Tom White, Ira Goldfine, Betty Maddox, Jack Youngren, and me. Betty and Jack had done the major laboratory work under Ira. We were ready to approach venture capital groups. Unfortunately, the timing was not good. It was at the time of the major crash as Mr. Obama took office. In spite of that, Tom was able to provide enough information, with presentations by Jack Youngren, that a number of venture capital groups proceeded with "due diligence" procedures.

There was a period of quiet. It became obvious that no one in the business knew who I was, so we had the good fortune to find that Kirk Robb, who had been CEO of Genentec, was willing to be chairman of our company. Here was a known name. When he recovered from an illness, things began to happen. A group of "angels," with the aid of a federal grant, provided us with a million dollars. With those funds, we believe that we can satisfy all those who have done due diligence. This development required that Ira, Betty, Jack, and I leave the board, making room for these new major investors. The four of us had received a major number of shares, with me getting the most.

The future is exciting, and I hope to live to see the success of our company, now named TriAct Therapeutics. The name came from the fact that we now have three drugs that show great promise, led by NDGA.

On the advice of a respected lawyer and friend, Maryellen Herringer, I have given each of my children a large number of shares.

Afterthoughts

Looking back on the eventful years after my return from combat in 1945, I feel blessed to have survived the horrors of combat. The first thought is of wife and children, who I feel have helped make my world a better place.

As a physician, it was my good fortune to be able to contribute to the improvement in the health care of women. I believe that helping in the development of the vaginal smear as a means of detecting cancer, and especially pre-cancer, has saved thousands of lives. Developments in that area continue. It was a great pleasure to be part of a program that gave women a wide choice in the way they had their children, and that also provided them with increase safety and comfort. If they decided that they did not want to continue with pregnancy, they were given safe ways to terminate.

There was special satisfaction in being able to help to control the costs of malpractice insurance in California. That made it possible for our profession to provide better health care. It was not required that physicians had to chose a specialty because its overhead was less.

It has been a joy for me, at this late time in my life, to be involved in the development of a new anti-cancer drug that offers great promise in many areas with a new approach to the treatment of that dread group of diseases. It also was possible for me to help establish a protocol for the development of new drugs at UCSF.

The French Legion of Honor—including the wonderful associated events: President Sarkozy's presentation of the medal, the reception, the visit to the joint session of the US Congress, the luncheon at the French consulate, having my children there, and the splendid article in the San Francisco Chronicle—were unexpected icing on the cake to a wonderful life.

The exciting experience of forming a new company late in my life was also unexpected.

What wonderful people I have met along the way.

From my youth, I abhorred war as a way to solve the problems of the world, and while serving as a combat medic, my feeling was emphatically confirmed. The contrast between the battlefield and the life I was blessed to live after I came home emphasizes the importance of picking leaders who exhaust all possibilities prior to going to war.

For sales, editorial information, subsidiary rights information or a
catalog, please write or phone or email:

iBooks
1230 Park Avenue, 9a
New York, NY 10128, US
Sales: 1-800-68-BRICK
Tel: 212-427-7139
www.BrickTowerPress.com
email: bricktower@aol.com

www.Ingram.com

CPSIA information can be obtained at www.ICGtesting.com
Printed in the USA
BVOW08s0113020715

406957BV00003B/195/P